Mathematics

THREE (EXTENSION)

FOR COMMON ENTRANCE

Answers

Mathematics

THREE (EXTENSION)

FOR COMMON ENTRANCE

Answers

Serena Alexander

GALORE PARK
AN HACHETTE UK COMPANY

About the author

Serena Alexander has taught mathematics since 1987, originally in both maintained and independent senior schools. From 1999 she taught at St Paul's School for Boys, where she was Head of mathematics at their Preparatory School, Colet Court, before moving first to Newton Prep as Deputy Head and then to Devonshire House as Head. She is now an educational consultant, with a focus on mathematics, and an ISI reporting inspector and in addition she helps to run regular mathematics conferences for prep school teachers.

Orders: please contact Bookpoint Ltd, 130 Milton Park, Abingdon, Oxon OX14 4SB. Telephone: (44) 01235 827720. Fax: (44) 01235 400454. Email education@bookpoint.co.uk Lines are open from 9 a.m. to 5 p.m., Monday to Saturday, with a 24-hour message answering service. Visit our website at www.galorepark.co.uk for details of other revision guides for Common Entrance, examination papers and Galore Park publications.

ISBN: 978 1 4718 4686 1

First published in 2015 by

Galore Park Publishing Ltd,

An Hachette UK Company

Carmelite House

50 Victoria Embankment

London EC4Y 0DZ

www.galorepark.co.uk

Impression number 10 9 8 7 6 5 4 3 2 1

Year 2019 2018 2017 2016 2015

Illustrations by Integra Software Services Pvt. Ltd.

Some illustrations by Graham Edwards were re-used. The publishers will be pleased to make the necessary arrangements with regard to these illustrations at the first opportunity.

Typeset in India

Printed and bound by CPI Group (UK) Ltd, Croydon, CR0 4YY

A catalogue record for this title is available from the British Library.

Contents

Introduction

This book provides a complete set of answers to the questions in *Mathematics for Common Entrance Three (Extension)*.

For some questions and activities, pupils are asked to copy diagrams from the book. They may find tracing paper helpful when doing this.

Setting out work

Pupils are individuals and no two will present work in exactly the same way. However, it is important to set basic ground rules for presentation, as keeping their calculations neat and clear will help pupils to avoid mistakes. It will also enable you to see what they are doing.

For simple arithmetic:

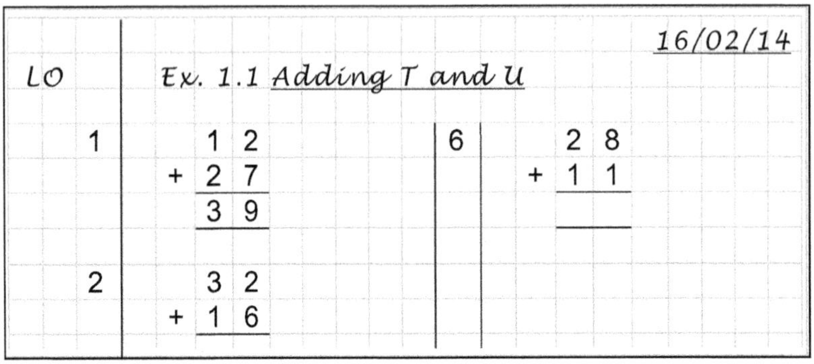

For more complex problems, encourage the 'saucepan' shape to setting out chains of calculations.

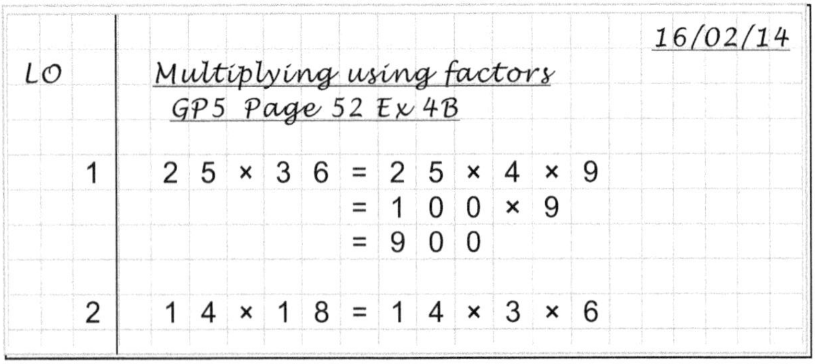

1 Working with numbers

Exercise 1.1

1 35	7 96	13 6	19 120	25 39
2 72	8 198	14 225	20 28	26 448
3 159	9 14	15 76	21 175	27 214
4 6	10 28	16 196	22 401	28 168
5 31	11 440	17 516	23 25	29 524
6 111	12 45	18 53	24 319	30 57
31 650	37 520	43 15	49 640	55 225
32 18	38 63	44 114	50 360	56 225
33 106	39 210	45 171	51 180	57 500
34 809	40 816	46 181	52 24	58 10 000
35 315	41 39	47 475	53 169	59 40
36 20	42 5	48 792	54 225	60 1250

Exercise 1.2

1 972	6 331 968	11 14 697	16 99 495
2 4263	7 404 928	12 27	17 22.4
3 18 283	8 217	13 75 964	18 27
4 23	9 215 r 6	14 375	19 51 085
5 43	10 206 r 12	15 90 090	20 27.5

Exercise 1.3

1 8760 hours
2 10 080 minutes, 604 800 seconds
3 1568 ounces
4 9680 yards
5 2992 beef burgers
6 440 pints

7 22 classes

8 (a) 368 sheets

(b) 15 minutes 20 seconds

9 (a) £2327.50

(b) £848.50

10 8p

Exercise 1.4

1 $^{-}7$

2 $^{-}3$

3 $^{-}3$

4 16

5 $^{-}9$

6 $^{-}3$

7 $^{-}22$

8 $^{-}21$

9 $^{-}4$

10 3

11 $^{-}12$

12 17

13 6

14 $^{-}12$

15 4

16 $^{-}10$

17 $^{-}4$

18 12

19 $^{-}5$

20 25

21 $^{-}5$

22 4

23 $^{-}12$

24 $^{-}2$

25 $^{-}1$

26 $^{-}7$

27 5

28 16

29 $^{-}3$

30 $^{-}10$

Exercise 1.5

1 5, 17, 37

2 1, 2, 3, 4, 6, 9, 36

3 12, 24, 36

4 (a) 2, 3, 7

(b) 2, 5

5 17

6 (a) 84

(b) 16

(c) 42

7 31, 37, 41, 43, 47,

8 (a) 1, 5, 13, 65

(b) 1, 101

(c) 1, 19

(d) 1, 2, 3, 4, 6, 8, 9, 12, 18, 24, 36, 72

9 (a) $2^3 \times 3^2 \times 7$

(b) $2^3 \times 17$

(c) $2^3 \times 5^3$

(d) $3^3 \times 5 \times 7$

10 (a) 1, 2, 3, 4, 6, 8, 12, 24; 1, 2, 3, 6, 7, 14, 21, 42

(b) 1, 2, 3, 6

(c) 6

11 (a) 2

(b) 10

(c) 20

12 4, 8, 12, 16, 20, 24, 28, 32, 36, 40

13 6, 12, 18, 24, 30, 36, 42, 48, 54, 60

14 10, 20, 30, 40, 50, 60, 70, 80, 90, 100

15 (a) 12

(b) 20

(c) 30

16 (a) 40

(b) 60

(c) 1800

Exercise 1.6

1 (a) 63
(b) 8
(c) 5
(d) 1

2 5

3 33

4 58

5 200

6 120

7 (a) 7560
(b) 8568
(c) 189 000
(d) 128 520

8 11 550

9 660

10 8932

11 180

12 (a) 28, 56, 84, 112
(b) 300

Exercise 1.7

1 8

2 22

3 2

4 20

5 111

6 35

7 401

8 13

9 117

10 8

Extension Exercise 1.8

1 8

2 15

3 105

4 135

5 135

6 125

7 1

8 196

9 21

10 16

11 54

12 325

13 100

14 $\frac{1}{8}$

15 4

16 28

17 1.5

18 $2\frac{1}{4}$

19 13

20 27

Summary Exercise 1.9

1 85

2 124

3 96

4 12

5 493

6 186

7 432

8 29

9 444

10 23

11 (a) $^{-}11$

(b) 11

(c) 12

(d) $^{-}7$

(e) 8

(f) $^{-}5$

(g) $^{-}75$

(h) $^{-}3$

(i) $^{-}12$

(j) 3

12 5, 13, 31

13 1, 2, 4, 7, 14, 28

14 6, 12, 30

15 (a) 8

(b) 42

16 (a) 40

(b) 1848

17 Yes, 2579 kg

18 (a) 2068 kg

(b) 22 days ($22\frac{1}{2}$ days almost)

Activity: Largest and smallest sums and differences

This sounds very simple, but working out where to put the digits requires a thorough understanding of place value.

Smallest sum	Largest sum	Smallest difference	Largest difference
78 + 69 = 147	96 + 87 = 183	86 − 79 = 7	98 − 67 = 31
579 + 468 = 1047	964 + 875 = 1839	745 − 698 = 47	987 − 456 = 531
3579 + 2468 = 6047	9753 + 8642 = 18 395	6234 − 5987 = 247	9876 − 2345 = 7531
02 468 + 13 579 = 16 047	97 531 + 86 420 = 183 951	50 123 − 49 876 = 247	98 765 − 01 234 = 97 531

Check pupils' comments on the numbers they have produced.

2 Fractions and decimals

For those pupils who are interested Ancient Egyptians and their fractions provide many opportunities for research. The Horus fractions are considered 'magic' but your pupils are probably more familiar with the magic number $9\frac{3}{4}$. *It could be a special challenge to find the 5 questions to which* $9\frac{3}{4}$ *is the answer.*

Exercise 2.1

1 (a) $\frac{1}{4}=\frac{2}{8}$ (b) $\frac{12}{16}=\frac{3}{4}$ (c) $\frac{2}{5}=\frac{4}{10}$ (d) $\frac{9}{24}=\frac{3}{8}$

2 (a) $9\frac{3}{4}$ (b) $2\frac{2}{5}$ (c) $3\frac{1}{2}$ (d) $10\frac{2}{3}$

3 (a) $\frac{21}{5}$ (b) $\frac{15}{4}$ (c) $\frac{39}{5}$ (d) $\frac{22}{7}$

4 (a) $\frac{3}{5}$ (b) $\frac{2}{3}$ (c) $\frac{7}{18}$ (d) $\frac{3}{7}$

5 (i) (a) 0.15 (b) 0.24 (c) 0.56 (d) 1.25

(ii) (a) $\frac{3}{20}$ (b) $\frac{6}{25}$ (c) $\frac{14}{25}$ (d) $1\frac{1}{4}$

6 (i) (a) $\frac{7}{20}$ (b) $1\frac{9}{25}$ (c) $\frac{2}{25}$ (d) $\frac{1}{8}$

(ii) (a) 35% (b) 136% (c) 8% (d) 12.5%

7 (i) (a) 0.4 (b) 0.56 (c) 0.65 (d) 0.625

(ii) (a) 40% (b) 56% (c) 65% (d) 62.5%

8 (a) (i) $0.\dot{3}$ (ii) $\frac{1}{3}$

(b) (i) $0.8\dot{3}$ (ii) $\frac{5}{6}$

(c) (i) $0.\dot{4}$ (ii) $\frac{4}{9}$

(d) (i) $1.\dot{4}\dot{5}$ (ii) $1\frac{5}{11}$

9 (a) (i) $0.\dot{6}$ (ii) $66\frac{2}{3}\%$

(b) (i) $0.\dot{7}$ (ii) $77\frac{7}{9}\%$

(c) (i) $0.1\dot{6}$ (ii) $16\frac{2}{3}\%$

(d) (i) $3.\dot{1}42\,85\dot{7}$ (ii) $314\frac{2}{7}\%$

10 (a) $\frac{1}{5}$ (b) $\frac{3}{10}$ (c) $\frac{7}{40}$

(d) 7.5% (e) 9% (f) 12.5%

Some teachers may prefer their pupils to turn mixed numbers into improper fractions when adding or subtracting. This does work but can give some very unwieldy numbers, making such calculations without a calculator very difficult.

Encourage pupils to look for lowest common denominators and not just multiply the two denominators together.

Exercise 2.2

1 $\frac{13}{15}$

2 $\frac{7}{8}$

3 $\frac{5}{24}$

4 $\frac{1}{4}$

5 $1\frac{11}{36}$

6 $\frac{7}{30}$

7 $4\frac{11}{12}$

8 $6\frac{4}{15}$

9 $3\frac{1}{20}$

10 $\frac{4}{63}$

11 $7\frac{15}{16}$

12 $3\frac{3}{10}$

13 $2\frac{7}{12}$

14 $5\frac{8}{15}$

15 $2\frac{22}{35}$

16 $\frac{7}{10}$

17 $9\frac{3}{4}$

18 $7\frac{25}{42}$

19 $1\frac{13}{24}$

20 $1\frac{7}{30}$

Exercise 2.3

Remind pupils of the BIDMAS rule.

1 $\frac{31}{60}$

2 $\frac{23}{45}$

3 $1\frac{1}{20}$

4 $\frac{13}{60}$

5 $\frac{43}{60}$

6 $\frac{71}{84}$

7 $1\frac{13}{60}$

8 $\frac{1}{20}$

9 $\frac{11}{60}$

10 $\frac{53}{60}$

11 $1\frac{23}{60}$

12 $\frac{5}{8}$

13 $\frac{1}{40}$

14 $3\frac{31}{40}$

15 $9\frac{3}{4}$

16 $2\frac{19}{20}$

17 $1\frac{47}{60}$

18 $\frac{11}{20}$

Exercise 2.4

This is a good exercise to do before going on to multiplication. It also provides a little revision of units.

1 5

2 6

3 12

4 30

5 54

6 65

7 115

8 57.6

9 75

10 99

11 60.5 km

12 136 m

13 80.5 miles

14 120 cm

15 80 minutes

16 2250 g

17 4 km 571 m

18 2 hours 30 minutes

19 4800 mm

20 25 seconds

Exercise 2.5

1 $\frac{4}{7}$
2 $\frac{2}{7}$
3 $1\frac{1}{9}$
4 $2\frac{11}{12}$
5 $\frac{1}{6}$
6 $\frac{2}{9}$
7 $1\frac{1}{3}$
8 $\frac{3}{4}$
9 $\frac{1}{9}$
10 $2\frac{2}{3}$
11 $\frac{1}{2}$
12 $\frac{11}{12}$
13 $\frac{4}{5}$
14 $1\frac{11}{12}$
15 $9\frac{3}{4}$
16 $^{-}8\frac{1}{8}$
17 $^{-}9$
18 $^{-}1\frac{7}{39}$
19 3
20 $\frac{32}{55}$
21 $\frac{8}{45}$
22 $\frac{3}{50}$
23 $\frac{11}{150}$
24 $\frac{1}{18}$
25 16
26 12
27 $9\frac{3}{4}$
28 4
29 $42\frac{13}{144}$
30 $388\frac{4}{5}$

Exercise 2.6

1 $2\frac{13}{15}$
2 $\frac{5}{7}$
3 $\frac{1}{2}$
4 $4\frac{17}{70}$
5 $2\frac{1}{8}$
6 $\frac{15}{61}$
7 $\frac{37}{40}$
8 $\frac{5}{8}$
9 $9\frac{3}{4}$
10 $2\frac{80}{111}$

Exercise 2.7

1 $6\frac{1}{12}$ m
2 $5\frac{1}{24}$ m
3 $\frac{3}{4}$ m
4 $\frac{5}{24}$ kg
5 $1\frac{2}{27}$
6 $2\frac{1}{10}$ km

7 $\frac{5}{12}$ of the class are girls that do not wear glasses. 24 is the smallest number of pupils in the class (although from this fraction the class could be 12, but $\frac{3}{8}$ of 12 is not a whole number).

8 (a) $1\frac{13}{24}$ miles (b) $4\frac{7}{18}$ miles (c) $10\frac{71}{72}$ miles

Exercise 2.8

1 0.24
2 60
3 0.000 12
4 $^{-}30$
5 $^{-}0.1$
6 4
7 $^{-}0.078$
8 1.56
9 3000
10 30 000
11 $^{-}1.68$
12 0.378
13 $^{-}3.4$
14 0.2
15 640
16 24
17 40 000
18 $^{-}0.67$
19 $^{-}0.002$
20 0.002

Exercise 2.9

1 £54
2 £3.80
3 £8.22
4 £65
5 £5.90
6 42p
7 £1.47
8 11, 65p
9 £15.90
10 £166.70
11 £6.60
12 £2.90
13 £23.61
14 £4.80

Exercise 2.10

1 20 cl
2 80 boys
3 600 000
4 Both 14 km (14 000 m)
5 54.6 cm
6 500 ml of shampoo costing £2.25 (45p per ml rather than 50p per ml)
7 1500 km
8 3
9 2382 mm
10 640 litres

Exercise 2.11

1 0.1 m by 10 m, 0.4 m by 2.5 m, 0.25 m by 4 m,
0.125 m by 8 m, 0.8 m by 1.25 m, 0.5 m by 2 m, other answers are possible
2 0.1 m by 20 m, 0.2 m by 10 m, 0.25 m by 8 m,
0.4 m by 5 m, 0.8 m by 2.5 m, other answers are possible

3 8 m

4 0.2 cm

5 0.3 m

6 $0.24 m^2$

7 4 cm

8 5.333 or $5\frac{1}{3}$ cm

9 1000 cm (10 m)

10 192 cm (1.92 m)

Exercise 2.12

1 (a) 500	(b) 516.2	(c) 516	(d) 516.153
2 (a) 0.14	(b) 0.14	(c) 0.1365	(d) 0.1365
3 (a) 9	(b) 9.4	(c) 9.36	(d) 9.357
4 (a) 0.08	(b) 0.1	(c) 0.083 28	(d) 0.0833
5 (a) 2	(b) 2.0	(c) 2.00	(d) 2.000
6 (a) 11	(b) 10.9	(c) 10.91	(d) 10.909

These following questions and their answers are intended to open up discussion.

7 0.22 m, so 22 cm

8 8, 8 and 9

9 About 133 ml

10 9 days

11 If the sand is divided equally then each house will get just over 833 kg. But it does not say equal so the amount could vary.

12 3 m

13 221 ml

14 1.6 million

15 £67.15

Extension Exercise 2.13

1 $\frac{63}{64}$

2 $\frac{1}{64}$

3 (a) $\frac{1}{4}$	(b) $\frac{1}{8}$	(c) $\frac{1}{16}$	(d) $\frac{1}{32}$

4 (a) $\frac{1}{16}$ (b) $\frac{1}{8}$ (c) $\frac{1}{64}$ (d) $\frac{1}{4}$

5 Note that $\frac{1}{4}+\frac{1}{4}=\frac{1}{2}$ is allowed but $2\times\frac{1}{4}=\frac{1}{2}$ is not.

There are many different answers. You could get pupils to check each others' answers by using a calculator.

6 (a) $\frac{1}{2}+\frac{1}{8}$ (b) $\frac{1}{2}+\frac{1}{16}$ (c) $\frac{1}{2}+\frac{1}{8}+\frac{1}{32}$ (d) $\frac{1}{4}+\frac{1}{8}+\frac{1}{64}$

7 (a) $\frac{1}{4}\div\left(\frac{1}{2}+\frac{1}{4}\right)$ (c) $\left(\frac{1}{4}+\frac{1}{8}+\frac{1}{16}\right)\div\left(\frac{1}{2}+\frac{1}{16}\right)$

(b) $\left(\frac{1}{4}+\frac{1}{8}\right)\div\left(\frac{1}{2}+\frac{1}{8}\right)$ (d) $\left(\frac{1}{4}+\frac{1}{16}+\frac{1}{32}\right)\div\left(\frac{1}{2}+\frac{1}{8}+\frac{1}{32}\right)$

8 Find the smallest multiple of 2 that is larger than a or b. Then the calculation will be $\frac{a}{2^n}\div\frac{b}{2^n}$

You then need to find a number of different multiples of 2 which add up to a and b. This is where a table might help.

Summary exercise 2.14

1 (a) $2\frac{5}{24}$ (b) $6\frac{1}{10}$ (c) 15 (d) $1\frac{1}{5}$

2 (a) 0.12 (b) 0.03 (c) 0.02 (d) 60

3 $\frac{9}{80}$

4 14.08

5 $23\frac{1}{9}$ m

6 (a) 0.22 m^2 (b) 800 cm

7 (a) (i) 4.25 (ii) 4.255

(b) (i) 12.05 (ii) 12.046

(c) (i) 4.01 (ii) 4.010

8 (a) (i) 140 000 (ii) 143 000

(b) (i) 0.046 (ii) 0.0457

(c) (i) 50 000 (ii) 50 000

9 (a) $3\frac{3}{8}$ kg (b) 0.9 kg (900 g)

Activity: The National Elf problem

This is an interesting investigation as it does not give a simple answer but requires pupils to explore the relationship with highest common factors. It is worth guiding your pupils to carry out a structured investigation of different sized rectangles before they attempt to look for a rule or formula.

Plenty of discussion to be encouraged here!

(a) 2 (b) 6 (c) 16

(d) If $x = y$ then there are x elves.

If y is a factor of x then there are x elves.

9 by 6	$9 + 6 = 15$	HCF 3	Number of elves 12	(15 – 3)
4 by 6	$4 + 6 = 10$	HCF 2	Number of elves 8	(10 – 2)
12 by 8	$12 + 8 = 20$	HCF 4	Number of elves 16	(20 – 4)
15 by 12	$15 + 12 = 27$	HCF 3	Number of elves 24	(27 – 3)

3 Using a calculator

Exercise 3.1

1 Practical, just involves turning the calculator on.

2 61

3 22 008

4 0.040 404...

5 18 817 344

Exercise 3.2

1 $^{-}29$

2 As exercise 1.4

Exercise 3.3

1 (a) 45	(c) 26	(e) 2	
(b) 54	(d) $^{-}10$	(f) 0.2	
2 (a) 380	(b) 81	(c) 52	(d) 4

Exercise 3.4

1 $24\frac{1}{2}$ 2 $\frac{1}{4}$ 3 $\frac{1}{5}$ 4 $\frac{1}{2}$

Exercise 3.5

1 (a) 9	(b) 343	(c) 6561	(d) 243
2 (a) 28	(b) 12	(c) 5	(d) 7

3 0.125, 8, 0.125, 8, ...

Exercise 3.6

1 17, 34, 51, 68, 85, 102, ...

2 15, 16, 17, 18

3 11, 12, 13

4 (a) A (4704) (b) B (3039.75) (c) B (2928)

5 (a) Too big, last digit should be 3
(b) Too big, last digit should be 2
(c) Too small, last digit should be 3 or 8
(d) Too small, last digit should be 9

6 (a) $321 \times 6 = 1926$
(b) $1234 + 692 = 1926$
(c) $80\,892 \div 42 = 1926$
(d) $214 \times 9 = 1926$

7 On the 10 001th time you will have 100 020 001

8 On the 1001th time you will have 1 002 001

9 Yes 3

10 524 288

Exercise 3.7

These answers are the same as those of questions 1–5 in Exercises 2.1–2.8 but done on the calculator.

You might suggest that pupils use their calculators to find other calculations where the answer is $9\frac{3}{4}$

Exercise 3.8

Pupils should give their estimates first and then calculate the accurate answers using their calculators.

1 5, 4.81

2 6000, 6210

3 0.05, 0.0523

4 0.02, 0.022

5 600, 591

6 3000, 3630

7 0.3, 0.313

8 600, 530

9 0.005, 0.006 03

10 400, 509

11 300, 343

12 2, 2.26

Exercise 3.9: Star challenge

SOB $80\{30^2 + 3 \times (106 - 69)\} = 80\,880$ is BOBBO

BOSS $4 \times \{9 \times (119 + 14) + 100\} = 5188$ is SIBB

BIBI = $\frac{50(26^2 - 13)}{13 \times 17} = 150$ is ISO

BOBBO $9^2(9^2 + 4^2 + 2^2) = 8181$ is BIBI

ISIS $(29 + 16) \times (81 + 98) = 8055$ is BOSS

ISO $\frac{135 \times 101}{3 \times 9}$ is SOS

EARTH $5 \times (26 + 42) + 25 \times (29 + 18) = 1515$ is ISIS

SIBB $\frac{100^2 + 3 \times 30^2}{\sqrt{625}} = 508$ is SOB

Earth to ISIS to BOSS to SIBB to SOB to BOBBO to BIBI and finally to ISO where the message is SOS.

Extension Exercise 3.10

1 (a) 5 (b) 1 (c) 0.04

2 4

3 Most are recurring decimals – but $\frac{1}{77}$ and $\frac{1}{121}$ are very interesting.

$\frac{1}{11}$ $0.\dot{0}\dot{9}$	$\frac{1}{55}$ $0.0\dot{1}\dot{8}$	$\frac{1}{99}$ $0.\dot{0}\dot{1}$
$\frac{1}{22}$ $0.0\dot{4}\dot{5}$	$\frac{1}{66}$ $0.0\dot{1}\dot{5}$	$\frac{1}{110}$ $0.00\dot{9}\dot{0}$
$\frac{1}{33}$ $0.\dot{0}\dot{3}$	$\frac{1}{77}$ $0.\dot{0}1\dot{2}\dot{9}8\dot{7}$	$\frac{1}{121}$ 0.008 26446281…
$\frac{1}{44}$ $0.02\dot{2}\dot{7}$	$\frac{1}{88}$ $0.011\dot{3}\dot{6}$	$\frac{1}{132}$ $0.00\dot{7}\dot{5}$

4 $\frac{1}{3} + \frac{1}{4} + \frac{1}{60}$

5 1, 0.5, 0.667, 0.6. 0.625, 0.615, 0.619, 0.618, 0.618, 0.618

6 (a) $\frac{1}{10}$ full

(b) $\frac{1}{5}$ full

(c) (i) $\frac{3}{10}$ full

(ii) $\frac{3}{5}$ full

(d) Just over 3 minutes (3 minutes 20 seconds) or $3\frac{1}{3}$ minutes

7 $\frac{xy}{x+y}$

8 The tank will fill in 3 minutes 36 seconds so it is to hoped that the intergalactic traveller managed to get his mask on first, although he may have had to hold his breath once the water level came over his mouth.

Summary exercise 3.11

1 283.41

2 31.924

3 104.419

4 (a) $1\frac{32}{195}$ (b) $1\frac{17}{63}$ (c) $4\frac{72}{77}$ (d) $2\frac{89}{544}$

5 (a) $\frac{2}{5}$ (b) $5\frac{23}{52}$

6 (a) $\frac{47}{50}$ (b) $\frac{1}{50}$

7 (a) (i) 4 (ii) 100 (to 1 s.f.)

(b) (i) 4.398 751 982 (ii) 114.734 913 4

8 (a) 7735 or SELL (c) 3108808 or BOBBIE

(b) 0.553 or ESSO (d) 55178 or BLISS

9 Check pupils' own answers.

Activity: Calculator puzzles and games

Label the calculator

This could serve as a ready guide for pupils who cannot make sense of their manuals.

Guess the number

See if the pupils can uncover why this puzzle works.

Down to zero

This exercise tests the pupils' observations on factors. If they can divide then they will get their number down to zero more quickly.

Countdown

This game is just like the TV game.

Finding remainders

This game uses the same methods pupils should have used in Exercise 1.3

The instructions spell out exactly the method they have to follow.

4 Index numbers

Although the work in this chapter, on indices and roots, goes beyond the requirements of the syllabus, it does teach the students how to use a wide range of functions on their calculators. A better understanding of this will be of great benefit to all of them and they do enjoy it.

It is a good idea to do some work with square roots before the pupils go on to Chapter 10 on Pythagoras' theorem. This section will familiarise them with squares and with roots and make them even more proficient with the relevant calculator functions.

The final section on calculating with square roots is strictly for scholars only.

Exercise 4.1

1 (a) 3^5 (b) 7^7 (c) 6^{11} (d) 3^5 (e) 4^9 (f) 7^5

2 (a) 2^3 (b) 7^4 (c) 4^4 (d) 3^3 (e) 5 (f) 7^2

3 (a) 4^4 (b) 7 (c) 5^5 (d) 3^3 (e) 1 (f) 7^4

4 (a) 3^{10} (b) 5^2 (c) 7 (d) 3^0 (1) (e) 2^0 (1) (f) 7^0 (1)

5 (a) 3^6
(b) 8^3
(c) $6^7 \times 5^6$
(d) $7^2 \div 2^2$ or $(3\frac{1}{2})^2$
(e) $6^7 \div 5^2$
(f) 4^4
(g) 2^7
(h) $3^2 \times 5^3 \times 2^2$ (or $6^2 \times 5^3$)
(i) $7^6 \times 3^2$
(j) 3^3
(k) $6^5 \times 5^5$ (or 30^5)
(l) 5^7
(m) $4^8 \times 3^3 \times 5^2$
(n) 6^{10}
(o) 6^2

6 (a) $2^3 + 3^3$ (b) $7^0 (1)$ (c) 3×4^2 (d) 5^3 (e) 3×4^5 (f) 3×7^3

Exercise 4.2

1 (a) 2^{-3} (b) 9^{-2} or 3^{-4} (c) 3^{-3} (d) 8^{-2} or 2^{-6} (e) 2^{-5} (f) 4^{-3} or 2^{-6}

2 (a) $\frac{1}{8}$ (b) $\frac{1}{81}$ (c) $\frac{1}{27}$ (d) $\frac{1}{64}$ (e) $\frac{1}{32}$ (f) $\frac{1}{64}$

3 (a) 3^{-2} (b) 2^{-4} or 4^{-2} (c) 7^{-2} (d) 12^{-2} (e) 2^{-7} (f) 3^{-3} (g) 6^{-3} (h) 5^{-4}

4 (a) 3^{-3} (b) 7^{-2} (c) 6^{-3} (d) $3^0 (1)$ (e) 4^{-4} (f) 7^{-4}

5 (a) 2^3 (b) 7^4 (c) 4^{-4} (d) 3^3 (e) 5^{-1} (f) 7^{-2}

6 (a) $3^0 (1)$ (b) 4^4 (c) 6^{-2} (d) 3^7 (e) 4^{-1} (f) 7^{10}

7 (a) 4^4 (b) 7^{-3} (c) 5^5 (d) $3^1 (3)$ (e) 2^4 (f) $7^0 (1)$

8 (a) 4^9 (b) 7^9 (c) 1 (d) 3^{-1} (e) 2^{12} (f) 7^{10}

Exercise 4.3

1 $x = {}^{\pm}1$

2 $a = {}^{\pm}10$

3 $b = {}^{\pm}7$

4 $c = {}^{\pm}9$

5 $y = {}^{\pm}2$

6 $a = {}^{\pm}8$

7 $x = {}^{\pm}0.3$

8 $a = {}^{\pm}40$

9 $b = {}^{\pm}0.4$

10 $y = {}^{\pm}20$

11 $x = {}^{\pm}0.01$

12 $s = {}^{\pm}0.5$

Exercise 4.4

1 4

2 5

3 100

4 0.16

5 1.44

6 0.5

7 0.01

8 0.0001

9 0.06

10 1.1

11 (a) $\frac{1}{10}$ (b) 0.1

12 (a) $\frac{1}{100}$ (b) 0.01

13 (a) $\frac{1}{3}$ (b) $0.\dot{3}$

14 (a) $\frac{1}{4}$ (b) 0.25

15 (a) $\frac{4}{9}$ (b) $0.\dot{4}$

16 (a) $\frac{2}{5}$ (b) 0.4

17 2

18 (a) $\frac{4}{9}$ (b) $0.\dot{4}$

19 (a) $\frac{4}{5}$ (b) 0.8

20 1

Exercise 4.5

1 (a) 1.4 (b) 2.6 (c) 4.5 (d) 9.9

2 (a) 6.93 (b) 10.9 (c) 15.8 (d) 100

3 (a) (i) 1.96
(ii) 1.9881
(iii) 1.301881
(b) 1.414
(c) $\sqrt{2} = ^{\pm}1.41$

4 (a) 2.71 (b) 3.16 (c) 3.47 (d) 1.00

5 (a) 2.64 (b) 3.98 (c) 5.91 (d) 7.48

Exercise 4.6

1 (a) $2025 = 3^4 \times 5^2$, 45
(b) $1089 = 3^2 \times 11^2$, 33
(c) $3136 = 2^6 \times 7^2$, 56
(d) $1521 = 3^2 \times 13^2$, 39
(e) $1225 = 5^2 \times 7^2$, 35
(f) $7056 = 2^4 \times 3^2 \times 7^2$, 84

2 (a) $64 = 2^6$, 4
(b) $125 = 5^3$, 5
(c) $216 = 2^3 \times 3^3$, 6
(d) $3375 = 3^3 \times 5^3$, 15
(e) $1728 = 2^6 \times 3^3$, 12
(f) $13824 = 2^9 \times 3^3$, 24

3 (a) 3 (b) 3 (c) 5 (d) 2 (e) 6 (f) 12

Exercise 4.7

1 (a) 10^4 (b) 10^3 (c) 10^{-3} (d) 10^{-6} (e) 10^{10} (f) 10^{-8}

2 (a) 3×10^4 (b) 4×10^{-5} (c) 9×10^{-2} (d) 6×10^{-4} (e) 7×10^{-8} (f) 8×10^7

3 (a) 200 (b) 0.000 06 (c) 700 000 000 (d) 2800 (e) 490 (f) 0.000 000 365

4 (a) 3.9×10^3 (b) 8.09×10^{11} (c) 2.005×10^{-7} (d) 6.075×10^5 (e) 3.9×10^4 (f) 9.08×10^6

5 (a) 5×10^{-3} (b) 6.84×10^{-3} (c) 3.2×10^{-5} (d) 8.09×10^{-7} (e) 5.4×10^{-1} (f) 1.909×10^{-5}

Exercise 4.8

1 4×10^{10}, 40 000 000 000

2 $3.155\,76 \times 10^9$, 3 155 760 000 seconds (allowing for leap years 365.25 days)

3 3.6×10^{10}, 36 000 000 000

4 4.8×10^7, 48 000 000

5 1.5×10^{-7}, 0.000 000 15

6 $3.142\,857\,1 \times 10^6$, £3 142 857.10

7 $1.666\,66 \times 10^9$, 1 666 666 667, £1.67×10^8, £166 666 667

8 3×10^4 mm, 1.8×10^4 mm, 1.36×10^{11} mg,

30 000 mm, 18 000 mm, 136 000 000 000 mg

9 2.2×10^4 mm/s, 22 222 mm/s

10 1136×10^6 mm/s $\div 60^2$, 315 555.56 mm/s

11 1.5×10^3, 1500

12 $2^{10} \times 2^{10} \times 4 \times 8$, 33 554 432, $3.355\,443\,2 \times 10^7$

13 (a) $300\,000 \times 60 \times 60 \times 24 \times 365 = 9.5 \times 10^{12}$ kilometres

(b) 4.07×10^{13}, 40 700 000 000 000

14 3.07×10^{13}, 30 700 000 000 000

15 4.5×10^9, 4 500 000 000

Extension Exercise 4.9

1 12
2 16
3 $\sqrt{3}\times\sqrt{7}$
4 6
5 $2\sqrt{2}$
6 $5\sqrt{5}$
7 18
8 $2\sqrt{14}$
9 $\sqrt{3}\times\sqrt{18}$ or $3\sqrt{6}$
10 12
11 $3\sqrt{3}$
12 $9\sqrt{2}$
13 $6\sqrt{2}$
14 $2\sqrt{15}$
15 8
16 15
17 $8\sqrt{3}$
18 $6\sqrt{5}$
19 12
20 $6\sqrt{15}$

Summary Exercise 4.10

1 (a) 3^3 (b) 2^6 (c) 4^5 (d) 7^3
2 (a) 27 (b) 64 (c) 1024 (d) 343
3 (a) 2^3 (b) 5^3 (c) 2^7 (d) 3^4 or 9^2
4 (a) $\frac{1}{4}$ (b) $\frac{1}{243}$ (c) $\frac{1}{343}$
5 (a) 3^6 (b) 7^3 (c) 3^{-3} (d) 2×3^3 (e) $5^2 \div 3^3$ (f) $3^3 \times 5^2$
6 (a) 4^{-1} (b) 3^1 or 3 (c) 4^{-4} (d) 2^2 (e) 5^{-4} (f) 7^0 or 1
7 (a) $x = \pm 4$ (b) $a = \pm 10$ (c) $b = \frac{1}{\sqrt{2}}$
8 (a) ± 4 (b) 1.21 (c) 0.09 (d) ± 0.2
9 (a) 70 000 (b) 2 750 000 (c) 0.000 15 (d) 0.009 702
10 (a) 4.7×10^4 (b) 8.1×10^{-3} (c) 5.06×10^8 (d) 4.02×10^{-4}
11 6 200 000 000, 6.2×10^9
12 (a) 5 (b) 3 (c) 12 (d) 70

Activity: Chain letters

1 3125
2 46 656
3 100 000
4 If x is the number of letters and y is the number on the list then the total is x^y
5 1×10^{10}, 10 000 000 000 (ten thousand million)
Population of Britain is approximately 60 000 000 (60 million).

5 Percentages

In this chapter, pupils revise the basic principles of percentages before moving on to percentage increases and decreases, finding the original amount and compound interest. Although the use of a calculator is essential for the majority of the chapter, it is important to ensure that pupils are recording their working in the correct manner.

A good rule to follow: Write down the calculation you are going to do before touching the buttons.

Exercise 5.1

1 (i) (a) 20% (c) 62.5%
(b) 30% (d) 16%
(ii) (a) 0.2 (c) 0.625
(b) 0.3 (d) 0.16

2 (i) (a) 0.14 (c) 0.33
(b) 0.65 (d) 0.44
(ii) (a) $\frac{7}{50}$ (c) $\frac{33}{100}$
(b) $\frac{13}{20}$ (d) $\frac{11}{25}$

3 (i) (a) $\frac{1}{8}$ (c) $\frac{1}{6}$
(b) $\frac{2}{3}$ (d) $\frac{3}{8}$
(ii) (a) 0.125 (c) 0.16
(b) 0.6 (d) 0.375

4 (i) (a) $\frac{1}{3}$ (b) $\frac{5}{6}$ (c) $\frac{2}{9}$
(ii) (a) $33\frac{1}{3}$% (b) $83\frac{1}{3}$% (c) $22\frac{2}{9}$%

5 12%

6 36%

7 £3.50

8 1.8 m

9 30 minutes

10 £1.75

11 315 km

12 44%

13 42p

14 (a) £22 (b) £30.80 (c) £35.20

15 60%

16 £5.75

17 £26.25

18 66%

19 £3.75

20 6 boxes, £11.40

Exercise 5.2

1 (a) Teddy bear, £2.40
(b) Tablet, £79
(c) Tennis racquet, £9.80
(d) Bicycle, £50
(e) Baseball cap, £1.90
(f) Football, £5

2 (a) Teddy bear, £14.40
(b) Tablet, £474
(c) Tennis racquet, £58.80
(d) Bicycle, £300
(e) Baseball cap, £11.40
(f) Football, £30

3 (a) T-shirt, £2.25
(b) Pencil case, 60p
(c) Wristwatch, £5.25
(d) Alarm clock, £1.80
(e) Sound system, £22.50
(f) Kettle, £3.75

4 (a) T-shirt, £12.75
(b) Pencil case, £3.40
(c) Wristwatch, £29.75
(d) Alarm clock, £10.20
(e) Sound system, £127.50
(f) Kettle, £21.25

5 £2.40

6 20%

7 4 balls for £3.60 gives 9% discount

8 14

Exercise 5.3

1 As last exercise question 2

2 As last exercise question 4

3 (a) 1.04
(b) 1.05
(c) 0.92
(d) 0.8
(e) 0.82
(f) 0.85
(g) 0.92
(h) 1.125
(i) 1.1
(j) 0.84
(k) 0.68
(l) 0.6 (you receive 0.6 (60%) of earnings)

4 £43.12

5 £28

6 £14.85

7 £441 000

8 £7225, £6502.50

9 24.4 m

10 4160 cm^3

Exercise 5.4

1 Original value: £25, new value: £22, decrease

2 Original value: £52.50, new value: £67.86, increase

3 Original value: £4500, new value: £3825, decrease

4 Original value: 416, new value: 395, decrease

5 Original value: £300, new value: £423, increase

6 Original value: £28 000, new value: £21 000, decrease

7 Original value: £50, new value: £160, increase

8 Original value: £220, new value: £190, decrease

9 Original value: £15, new value: £12, decrease

10 **1** Decrease 12%
2 Increase 29%
3 Decrease 15%
4 Decrease 5%
5 Increase 41%
6 Decrease 25%
7 Increase 320%
8 Decrease 14%
9 Decrease 20%

Exercise 5.5

1 £4700

2 £120

3 600 000

4 25 000

5 £35

6 2.4 litres

7 1.52 m

8 154

9 £7.20

10 £6800, £8000

Exercise 5.6

1 Original £375

2 New £3400

3 New £22 500

4 Original £1500

5 Original £42

6 New 63

7 Original 11p

8 Original 14 545 cm^3 or 14 litres (Correct rounding to 2 d.p. gives you 15 litres, but then the 10% extra will bring you over 16, therefore the answer has to be rounded down.)

Exercise 5.7

1 15%

2 £256.25

3 £600

4 £1750

5 £300 000

6 20%

7 £411 in January 2015, £400 in January 2014

The next question leads into compound interest.

8 (a) £146.85

(b) £166.51 The important thing here is that you cannot multiply your previous answer by 1.01

Extension Exercise 5.8

Once pupils have grasped the concept of compound interest this is a good exercise to show how spreadsheets can be used (especially question 4).

1 (a) £593.84 (b) £705.30 (c) £928.74 (d) £1029.71

2 (a) £6240 (b) £6749.18 (c) £7299.92

3 (a) (i) £9292.80 (ii) £6332.78 (iii) £3342.01

(b) £1440

(c) £455.73

4 (a) £25 525.63
(b) 15
(c) yes
(d) £110 000 (rounded)

5 (a) 8 years
(b) 35 years

6 In ten years' time (after sensible rounding)

(a) £10 590 (b) £570 (c) £16

Ten years ago

(a) £3890 (b) £210 (c) £6

7 (a)

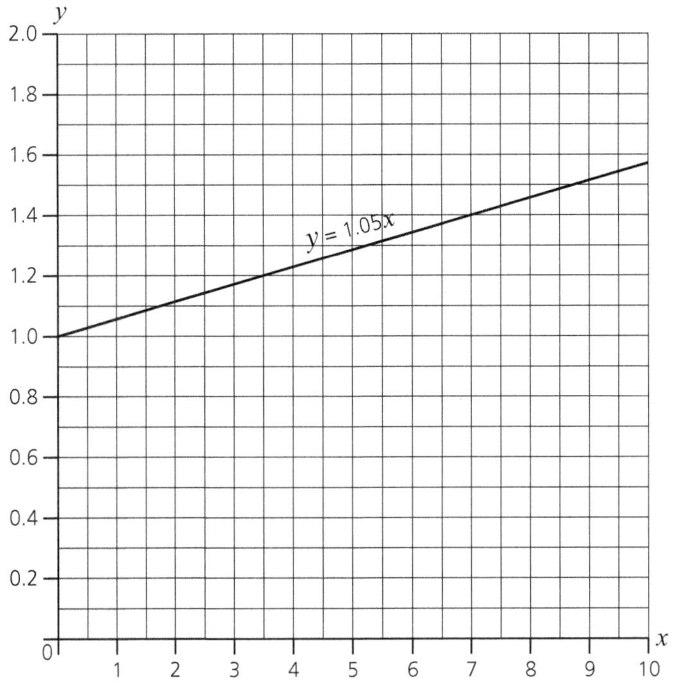

(b) (i) 4 and a half years
(ii) 8 and a half years
(iii) 6 years

(c) The answers do not depend on the original price of the goods at all because they are multiplied by $(1.05)^x$, (a) is when $(1.05)^x = 1.25$, (b) is when $(1.05)^x = 1.5$ and (c) is when $(1.05)^x = 1.33$

Summary Exercise 5.9

1 79%

2 1 hour and 52.5 minutes

3 271 kg

4 4.8%

5 (a) £131.25
(b) £15.73

6 (a) £472.50

(b) £12.50

(c) £166.67

7 £20

8 £387 000 (after sensible rounding)

9 16 minutes

10 £2152.80

Activity: Calculator maze

Various answers may be given. Possible answers are as follows.

(a) (i) The route to the highest amount is D C F G K O

(ii) The highest amount is £523.27

(b) (i) The route to £500 is C F G K O

(ii) The amount is £502.34

6 Equations and inequalities

Exercise 6.1

1 8	6 $^{-}24$	11 $\frac{2}{3}$	16 $1\frac{2}{9}$
2 7	7 $7\frac{1}{2}$	12 $^{-}1$	17 14
3 $1\frac{2}{3}$	8 $^{-}4$	13 $^{-}14$	18 7
4 32	9 1	14 $^{-}7$	19 $8\frac{2}{3}$
5 $1\frac{1}{5}$	10 $^{-}2$	15 0	20 $^{-}5\frac{1}{3}$

Exercise 6.2

1 (a) $a - 10$ (b) $a + 4$ (c) $a - 5$ (d) $a + 9$ (e) $a - 1$ (f) $a - 1$

2 $2(x - 1) = x + 9$, my age $x = 11$

3 (a) $4x$ (b) $x + 6$ (c) $4x + 6$

4 $3(x + 6) = 4x + 6$, my father is 48

5 (a) $y + 2$ (b) $4(y + 2)$ (c) $4(y + 2) = 5x$, I am 8

6 (a) (i) $3x$ (ii) $4x$

(b) $4x - 9 = 3x$ or $3x + 9 = 4x$, I am 9

7 (a) (i) $a - 4$ (ii) $a - 4$ (iii) $a - 8$

(b) $x - 4 = 2(x - 8)$, he is 8

8 12

9 16

10 12

Exercise 6.3

1 (a) (i) $c + 4$ (ii) $2(c + 4)$

(b) $3(c + 4) = 4c$, $c = 12$ (c) 32 ducklings

2 (a) (i) Red marbles $4y$ (ii) Green marbles $12y$

(b) $17y = 34$, yellow marbles $y = 2$

3 (a) (i) $x - 3$ (ii) $2x$

(b) $4x - 3 = 21$, $x = 6$, my sister picked 3 kg

4 (a) (i) $f + 4$ (ii) $100f$ (iii) $200(f + 4)$

(b) $100f + 200(f + 4) = 2300$, profit on each Fidget and Widget 5p and 9p

5 (a) $1.1x = 35.2$, $x = 32$ cm

(b) $1.2x = 6$, $x = £5$

(c) $x \div 1.1 = 15$, $x = £16.50$

(d) $x \div 1.25 = 4$, $x = 5$ kg

6 $x + x + 5 = 195$, $x = 95$, so there are 95 girls and 100 boys

7 $8 + 4x + x + 1 + 3 = 24$, 2 hours 24 minutes

8 $5x - (15 + 0.75x) = 250$, 63 cars

9 $5 + 3x = 2 + 8x$, the mass of one measure of chemical A is 0.6 mg.

10 $18x + 100 = 20(x - 10)$, the average height of pupils in my class is 150 cm.

Equations with fractions

Many pupils find equations with fractions very off-putting, possibly fearing that they are going to get into tangled fraction arithmetic. Some initial examples, showing how to get rid of all the fractions in one simple multiplication, even before you start these exercises, can help to reassure the pupils that these equations are not so difficult.

Remind pupils to check their answers by substituting back into the equations. With fractional answers this can become quite difficult and the correct use of a calculator should be encouraged.

Exercise 6.4

1 12

2 12

3 10

4 8

5 10

6 $6\frac{1}{2}$

7 $^-5\frac{1}{3}$

8 $\frac{1}{2}$

9 $\frac{2}{5}$

10 2

Exercise 6.5

1 9

2 20

3 6

4 $^{-}3\frac{1}{2}$

5 $^{-}2$

6 $3\frac{1}{3}$

7 $^{-}21$

8 $1\frac{5}{7}$

9 $^{-}1\frac{1}{2}$

10 $1\frac{7}{13}$

11 $^{-}3\frac{1}{3}$

12 $1\frac{11}{12}$

13 $^{-}1\frac{1}{2}$

14 $\frac{1}{21}$

15 $^{-}1\frac{3}{4}$

16 $1\frac{5}{11}$

Exercise 6.6

1 3, 4, 5

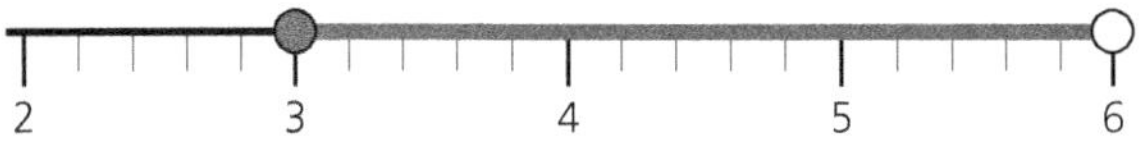

2 1, 2, 3, 4

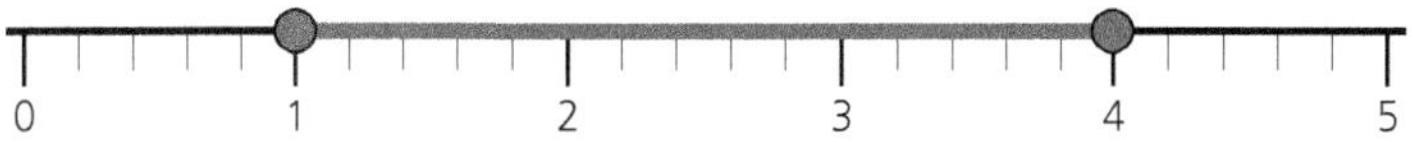

3 6, 7, 8

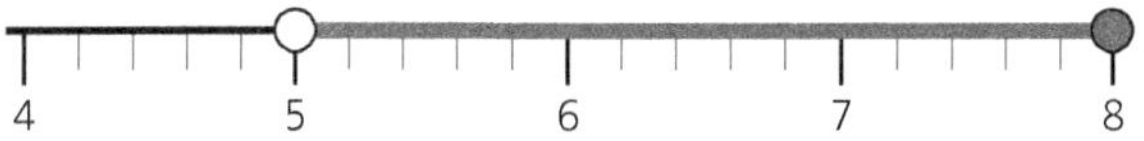

4 1, 2, 3, 4

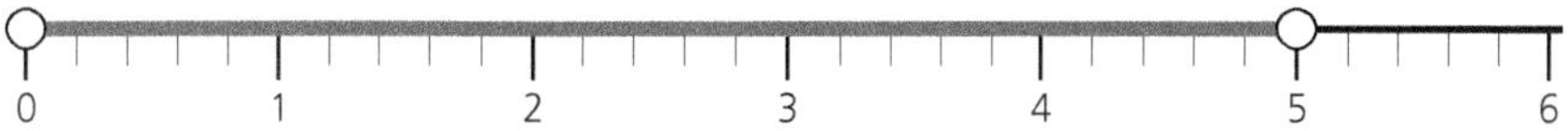

5 $^{-}2, ^{-}1, 0, 1, 2$

6 $^{-}7, ^{-}6$

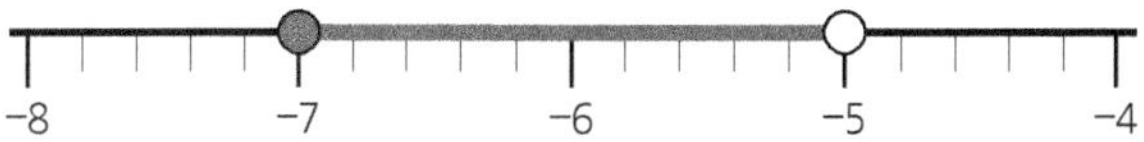

7 0, 1, 2, 3

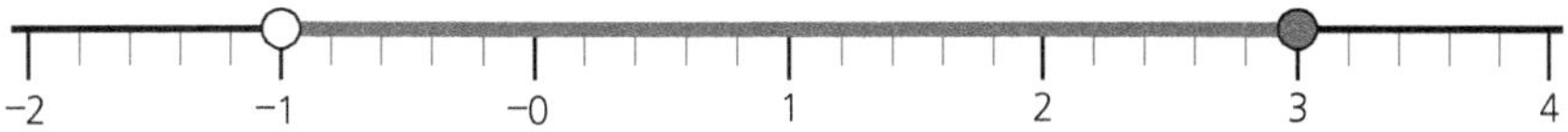

8 $^{-}1, 0, 1, 2$

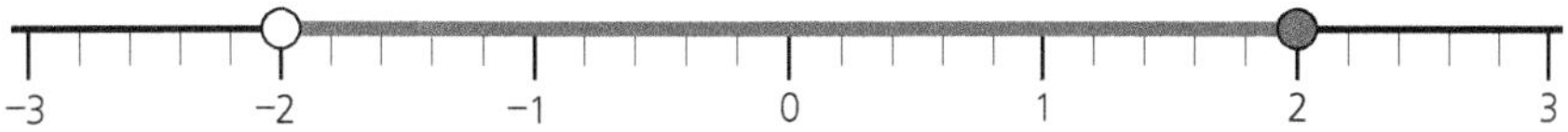

9 4, 5, 6, 7

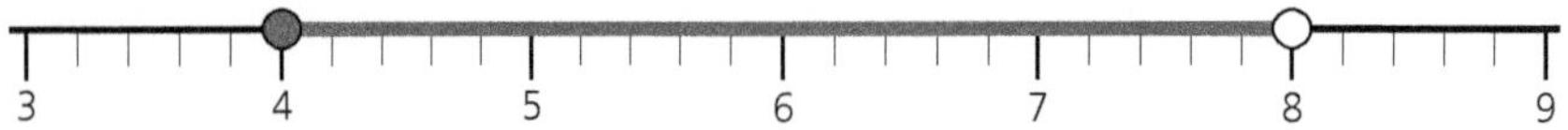

10 5, 6, 7, 8, 9

Exercise 6.7

1 $x < 2$

2 $y \geqslant 3$

3 $z \geqslant 3$

4 $x > 28$

5 $a \leqslant 7$

6 $b < 2$

7 $c < 1$

8 $s > \frac{2}{3}$

9 $t \geqslant 1$

10 $v > 11$

11 $x \leqslant 27$

12 $x > 0$

13 $x \leqslant 24$

14 $x \geqslant 10$

At this stage of equation solving, it is worth emphasising that it is better to keep the x-term positive. This is particularly true when solving inequalities. By keeping the x-term positive pupils do not have to worry about reversing the inequality.

Exercise 6.8

1 $x < \frac{1}{2}$

2 $x > ^{-}\frac{1}{2}$

3 $x \geqslant ^{-}\frac{4}{5}$

4 $x < 2\frac{2}{3}$

5 $x \geqslant ^{-}36$

6 $x > 6\frac{2}{3}$

7 $x \geqslant 1$

8 $x > 28$

9 $x \leqslant 9$

10 $x < 2$

11 $x \leqslant ^{-}3$

12 $x > 6\frac{2}{3}$

13 $x < 1\frac{1}{4}$

14 $x > 3$

15 $x \geqslant ^{-}1$

16 $x \geqslant 2\frac{6}{13}$

17 (a) 1 (0 is not normally regarded as a perfect square)

(b) 2

18 (a) 25 (b) 10 (c) 18 (d) 13 or 23

19 (a) $x < 3\frac{1}{2}$ (b) 2 and 3

20 (a) $x < ^{-}2$ (b) $^{-}3$

Extension Exercise 6.9

1 $\frac{3}{8}$

2 $\frac{8}{15}$

3 $\frac{14}{15}$

4 $1\frac{1}{9}$

5 $1\frac{11}{16}$

6 $2\frac{1}{2}$

7 24

8 15

9 $3\frac{5}{9}$

10 $-\frac{1}{7}$

11 $^{-}6$

12 $^{-}6\frac{2}{3}$

13 $4\frac{1}{2}$

14 $\frac{5}{69}$

Extension Exercise 6.10

1 (a) (i) True, 2 is greater than $1\frac{1}{2}$

(ii) False, they are equal.

(iii) True, 19 is greater than 5

(iv) False, 3 is not greater than $3\frac{1}{2}$

(v) True, 101 is greater than 100

(vi) False, 3 is not greater than $4\frac{1}{2}$

(b) **(iv)** x ▲ $2x - 1$ is always true.

(c) **(i)** x ▲ $x + 1$ is true when $x > 1$

(vi) x ▲ x^2 is true when $x < 2$

2 (a) (i) True, 4 is less than $3\frac{1}{2}$ plus 1

(ii) True, 3 is less than $2\frac{1}{2}$ plus 1

(iii) False, 7 is not less than $5\frac{1}{2}$ plus 1

(iv) False, 50 is not less than $25\frac{1}{2}$ plus 1

(v) False, 101 equals 100 plus 1

(vi) True, 5 is less than $12\frac{1}{2}$ plus 1

(b) (i) Not always true, only when $x < 3$

(ii) Always true $x < 2x$

(iii) $x < 2x + 1$ always true.

(iv) $x < 2x - 1$ not always true.

(v) $x < 2(x + 1)$ always true.

(vi) $x < x^2$ always true.

(c) (i) $x < x + 1$ is true when $x < 3$

(iv) $x < 2x - 1$ is true when $x < 1$

Summary Exercise 6.11

1 (a) 1

(b) $1\frac{1}{2}$

(c) $1\frac{2}{3}$

(d) $\frac{1}{2}$

(e) 5

(f) $^{-}3\frac{1}{3}$

2 (a) $3a$

(b) $a - 4$

(c) $3a - 4$

(d) $3a - 4 = 4(a - 4)$, $a = 12$

3 (a) $5x + 8$

(b) $4x + 12$

(c) $4x + 12 = 5x + 8$, $x = 4$

4 (a) $^{-}9$

(b) $4\frac{1}{2}$

(c) $2\frac{2}{3}$

(d) $2\frac{1}{2}$

(e) $6\frac{2}{3}$

(f) $5\frac{5}{8}$

5 (a) $x = 1, 2, 3, 4$

(b) $x = {}^{-}2, {}^{-}1, 0, 1$

6 (a) $x < 4$

(b) $x \geqslant 2\frac{1}{2}$

(c) $x \leqslant \frac{5}{6}$

Activity: Polyhedral numbers

1 You are adding triangular numbers.

2

n		Tertrahedral number
1	1	1
2	1 + 3	4
3	1 + 3 + 6	10
4	1 + 3 + 6 + 10	20
5	1 + 3 + 6 + 10 + 15	35
6	1 + 3 + 6 + 10 + 15 + 21	56
7	1 + 3 + 6 + 10 + 15 + 21 + 28	84
8	1 + 3 + 6 + 10 + 15 + 21 + 28 + 36	120
9	1 + 3 + 6 + 10 + 15 + 21 + 28 + 36 + 45	165
10	1 + 3 + 6 + 10 + 15 + 21 + 28 + 36 + 45 + 55	220
11	1 + 3 + 6 + 10 + 15 + 21 + 28 + 36 + 45 + 55 + 66	286

3 **(a)** 10th is 220

(b) 100th is 171 700

4 nth tetrahedral number is $\frac{n(n+1)(n+2)}{6}$

5 The next set of polyhedral numbers is one formed by square-based pyramids. The first such number will be 1, the second will be 1 + 4 = 5, the third 1 + 4 + 9, ...

n		Square-based pyramid number
1	1	1
2	1 + 4	5
3	1 + 4 + 9	14
4	1 + 4 + 9 + 16	30
5	1 + 4 + 9 + 16 + 25	55
6	1 + 4 + 9 + 16 + 25 + 36	91
7	1 + 4 + 9 + 16 + 25 + 36 + 49	140
8	1 + 4 + 9 + 16 + 25 + 36 + 49 + 64	204

10th is 385

100th is 338 350

nth square-based pyramid number is $\frac{n(n+1)(2n+1)}{6}$

n		Pentagon-based pyramid number
1	1	1
2	$1 + 5$	6
3	$1 + 5 + 12$	18
4	$1 + 5 + 12 + 22$	40
5	$1 + 5 + 12 + 22 + 35$	75
6	$1 + 5 + 12 + 22 + 35 + 51$	126
7	$1 + 5 + 12 + 22 + 35 + 51 + 70$	196
8	$1 + 5 + 12 + 22 + 35 + 51 + 70 + 92$	288

10th is 550

100th is 505 000

nth pentagon-based pyramid number is $\frac{n^2(n + 1)}{2}$

If you compare your sequences to Pascal's triangle you will see that the tetrahedral numbers form the diagonal under the triangle numbers, which is very satisfactory.

It would be good if the other polyhedral numbers were found here too but they are not. The diagonals in fact form a continuation of the pattern for the tetrahedral numbers:

$$\frac{(n + 1)(n + 2)(n + 3)(n + 4)}{2 \times 3 \times 4}$$

A good extension to this activity would be to see if you can find a three-dimensional sequence which would give the numerical sequence.

7 Indices in algebra

Some of these exercises go beyond Common Entrance into Scholarship level questions. Since scholarship papers vary between schools, it is important that you know the ISEB level that your pupils are expected to have covered.

Factorising quadratic equations, as this topic does appear on several scholarship syllabi, is covered in Chapter 15

Exercise 7.1

1 x^7
2 b^6
3 a^7
4 2^9
5 2^{a+b}
6 3^5
7 a^9
8 3^{a+b}
9 x^6
10 3^6
11 x^6
12 b^7
13 a^8
14 2^{x+y+1}
15 a^{x+y}
16 $2^a \times 3^b$
17 a^{2y+2}
18 xy^a
19 x^{x+y+1}
20 $(ab^2)^y$

Exercise 7.2

1 a
2 b^4
3 x^3
4 2^3
5 3^{x-y}
6 a
7 x^4
8 $5^0 = 1$
9 x^5
10 $a^0 = 1$
11 $4y^4$
12 x^{x-1}
13 $2x^{a-3}$
14 $\frac{a^{b-c}}{2}$

Exercise 7.3

1 2^{-3}
2 a^{-3}
3 x^{-3}
4 $x^0 = 1$
5 7^{a-b}
6 x^{-1}
7 b^{-4}
8 $a^0 = 1$
9 x^2

10 $a^2 \div b^2$ or $\left(\frac{a}{b}\right)^2$

11 $2x^{-1}$ or $\frac{2}{x}$

12 $\frac{1}{5a^3}$

13 $\frac{y^3}{3}$

14 $\frac{1}{4x^3}$

Exercise 7.4

Although this exercise goes beyond the Common Entrance syllabus, it promotes better understanding of index numbers.

1 3^8

2 2^6

3 x^6

4 a^{15}

5 $4b^6$

6 $243a^{15}$

7 4^{ab}

8 x^{m^2}

9 $9a^{2m}$

10 $2^m x^{m^2}$

11 3^{-2}

12 4^8

13 2^{-2}

14 $\frac{x^6}{27}$

15 a^4

16 $\frac{1}{27x^5}$

17 $8a^6$

18 16

19 $\frac{a^5}{3}$

20 $\frac{1}{27}$

Exercise 7.5

1 a^6

2 $6a^6$

3 $3b + b^2 + 2b^3$

4 $6b^2$

5 $6a^4b^4$

6 $8x^2y$

7 $3xy + x^2y$

8 $4xy + x^2y - xy^2$

9 $12a^3b^2c^2$

10 $2bc + a^2b + 4ac$

Exercise 7.6

1 $3ab$

2 $3a^2$

3 $3a^2$

4 $4y$

5 5

6 $\frac{3a^2}{5}$

7 $\frac{a^2}{8b^2}$

8 $\frac{1}{4m}$

9 $\frac{8y^2}{5x}$

10 $\frac{2b^4}{3c}$

11 $3xy$

12 $\frac{3a^2}{b}$

13 $\frac{3}{2x}$

14 $\frac{3ac^2}{2b}$

15 $\frac{3xy}{2z}$

Exercise 7.7

1 $2x^2 + x$

2 $3x^2 - x$

3 $4x - 3x^2$

4 $2x^2 + 8x$

5 $6x^2 - 15x$

6 $x^3 + x^2$

7 $x^3 + x^2 - x$

8 $4x^2 - 3x^3$

9 $6x^3 - 4x^2$

10 $2x^4 + 3x^3 + 4x^2$

11 $x^5 + x^3$

12 $6x^5 - 12x^4 + 9x^3$

Exercise 7.8

1 $4x^2 - 5x$

2 $x^2 + 8x$

3 $2x^2 + 2x$

4 $^{-}3x^2$

5 $4x^2 - 13x$

6 $4x^2 - 3x$

7 $9x^2 - 11x$

8 $^{-}x^2 - 7x$

9 $7x^2 - 2x$

10 $^{-}12x$

This last set of questions is good for those scholars who are going to have to deal with expanding brackets such as $(x - y)(x + y)$.

11 $x^2 + 2xy + y^2$

12 $6x^2 - 4y^2$

13 $2x^2 + 2xy + 2y^2$

14 $^{-}x^2y$

15 $5x^2 + 5xy$

16 $5x^2y^2 + 2xy^2 - 4x^2y$

17 $^{-}4x^2 - 5x^2y$

18 $3xy^2 - 6x^2y - x^2y^2$

19 $6x^4 - 15x^3y + 3x^3 - 8y$

20 $6x^3y + 2x^2y^2 - 9xy^3$

Exercise 7.9

1 $3(x + 2)$

2 $4(2y - 1)$

3 $3(2 + 3x)$

4 $2(9 - 2y)$

5 $8(3x + 2)$

6 $7x - 6$ Does not factorise.

7 $x(x + 5)$

8 $y(y - 7)$

9 $x(3 + x)$

10 $5x - y^2$ Does not factorise.

11 $x(x^2 + 2)$

12 $x^2(x - 3)$

13 $2x(x + 2)$

14 $3a(2 - 3a)$

15 $3y(3x + 2y - 1)$

16 $9a^2 - 8b$ Does not factorise.

17 $3x(4x - 3y + 2)$

18 $4a(2b - a)$

19 $x(3y + 16x + 4)$

20 $2ab(4a + 7)$

21 $8x^2 + 5y^2$ Does not factorise.

22 $3(4y^2 - 3y + x)$

23 $4y(3 + 2x^2 - 4y)$

24 $3a^2 + 6b^2 - 2ab$ Does not factorise.

25 $4xy(3 + 4x - y)$

26 $14x^2 + 8xy + 3y^2$ Does not factorise.

27 $2(5xy + 7y^2 - 2)$

28 $16x^2 - 12xy - 9$ Does not factorise.

29 $2x(8x - 7y - 3)$

30 $2b(10a^2 - 2ab - 1)$

31 $4ab(5a - b + 2)$

32 $2x(8y^2 + 4x - y)$

Exercise 7.10

1 $2 - y$

2 $x - 3xy$

3 $ab - 3a$

4 $u + 3v$

5 $\frac{9x-2y^2}{3}$

6 $2x - 3y$

7 $4a + b^2$

8 $\frac{cd+2d^2}{c}$

9 $p - 3q$

10 $\frac{5n-2m}{3}$

Trial and improvement

Pupils tend to read this as 'trial and error' but they should be encouraged to keep improving their answers. It is good practice to get into the routine of putting notes in the final column of the table. It will help pupils find the correct answer if they keep a note of 'too small' or 'too big' as they go along.

There can often be confusion about how far they should keep on searching. If the answer is to be given to 2 decimal places then they must work to 3 d.p.

Many pupils will assume that the closer answer is correct so it is worth putting the equations on a spreadsheet and graphing them, thus showing them that these are not linear relationships.

Exercise 7.11

1 (a) (i) 6.7 (ii) 6.72

(b) (i) 5.6 (ii) 5.64

(c) (i) 9.8 (ii) 9.77

2 (a) $h + 6$

(b) $h(h + 6)$

(c)

Height	Length	Area	Note
8	14	112	too small
9	15	135	too big
8.2	14.2	116.44	too small
8.3	14.3	118.69	too big
8.25	14.25	117.56...	too small

The height lies between 8.3 and 8.25 and therefore equals 8.3 cm to one decimal place.

3 (a) $b(b - 5)$

(b)

b	$b - 5$	Area	Note
10	5	50	too big
9	4	36	too small
9.2	4.2	38.64	too small
9.3	4.3	39.99	too small
9.4	4.4	41.36	too big
9.31	4.31	40.126	too big
9.305	4.305	40.058...	too big

The height lies between 9.3 and 9.305 and therefore equals 9.30 to 2 decimal places.

4 Length 9.4 m, width 7.4 m

5 Height 7.91 cm

6 8.94 m

7 9.6 cm and 12.6 cm

8 9.6 m

9 (a) $(x + 8)$

(b) $(x + 8)^2 - x^2$

(c) 115 mm

10 (a) Area = $\frac{x(2x+4)}{2} = x(x+2)$

(b)

x	$x+1$	$x+3$	Area	Note
3	4	6	15	too small
4	5	7	24	too big
3.5	4.5	6.5	19.25	too small
3.6			20.16	too big
3.58			19.976	too small
3.59			20.068	too big
3.585			20.022	too big

x lies between 3.58 and 3.585 and therefore the base equals 3.58 to 2 decimal places.

Extension Exercise 7.12

1 3

2 2

3 5

4 3

5 4

6 5

7 2

8 x

9 $2x$

10 $3x$

11 x^2

12 $\frac{1}{2x}$

Summary Exercise 7.13

1 (a) a^5 (b) b^5 (c) c^3d^2

2 (a) a^2 (b) b^3 (c) c^3

3 (a) a^{-2} (b) b^0 (c) c^{-4}

4 (a) $a^6 + a^5$ (b) $4b^3$ (c) $c^4 + c + c^2$

5 (a) $\frac{ab^2}{2}$ (b) $\frac{5ab}{c}$ (c) $\frac{9a^2}{2}$

6 (a) $x^2 + 3x$ (b) $6x^2 - 10x$ (c) $6x^2 - x^3$

7 (a) $4x^2 + x$ (b) $10x^2 - 28x$

8 (a) $3(x + 3)$

(b) $12x - 7$

(c) $2y(2x + y)$

(d) $3(x^2 - 4y)$

(e) $3(x^2 - 4x + 1)$

(f) $2(2x^2y - 4y^2 + 3x)$

(g) $y(12x^2 + 5y - 8)$

(h) $3x^2(3x - 2y + 5)$

9 x lies between 11.700 and 11.705 and therefore equals 11.70 to 2 decimal places.

Activity: Great Uncle Ben's bequest

The spreadsheet should come out like this.

Year	Scheme A	Total A	Scheme B	Total B	Scheme C	Total C	Scheme D	Total D
1	100	100	10	10	10.00	10.00	1	1
2	90	190	20	30	15.00	25.00	2	3
3	80	270	30	60	22.50	47.50	4	7
4	70	340	40	100	33.75	81.25	8	15
5	60	400	50	150	50.63	131.88	16	31
6	50	450	60	210	75.94	207.81	32	63
7	40	490	70	280	113.91	321.72	64	127
8	30	520	80	360	170.86	492.58	128	255
9	20	540	90	450	256.29	748.87	256	511
10	10	550	100	550	384.43	1133.30	512	1023

The answer really depends on how long you think Great Uncle Ben will live. Some pupils may investigate for more years, as you can see scheme D is rapidly overtaking scheme C.

The chart should look like this.

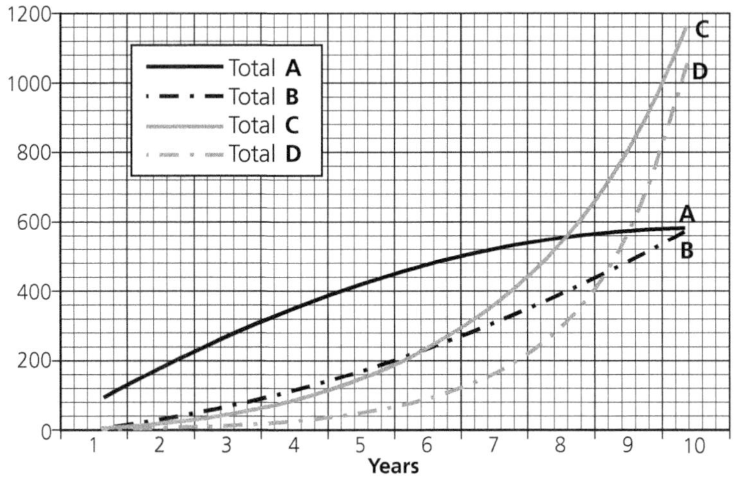

The great nephew's dilemma is to estimate how long Uncle Ben will live for. Scheme B is the safe option if he is not going to last more than 8 years. However if he is hale and hearty then scheme D will pay off best in 11 years and even more so in every year after that.

8 Sequences

Exercise 8.1

1	11, 13, 15	The rule is add 2
2	36, 49, 64	The rule is add increasing consecutive odd numbers.
3	18, 21, 24	The rule is add 3
4	21, 28, 36	The rule is add increasing counting numbers.
5	16, 19, 22	The rule is add 3
6	35, 48, 63	The rule is add increasing consecutive odd numbers.
7	21, 34, 55	The rule is add the last two terms.
8	16, 22, 29	The rule is add increasing consecutive numbers.
9	22, 26, 30	The rule is add 4
10	26, 31, 36	The rule is add 5

Exercise 8.2

1 (a)	**1**	1, 3, 5, 7, 9, ...	**(i)**	A table-based sequence
	2	1, 4, 9, 16, 25, ...	**(ii)**	A square number type sequence
	3	3, 6, 9, 12, 15, ...	**(i)**	A table-based sequence
	4	1, 3, 6, 10, 15, ...	**(iii)**	A triangular number type sequence
	5	1, 4, 7, 10, 13, ...	**(i)**	A table-based sequence
	6	0, 3, 8, 15, 24, ...	**(ii)**	A square number type sequence
	7	1, 1, 2, 3, 5, 8, 13, ...	**(iv)**	A Fibonnaci-style sequence
	8	1, 2, 4, 7, 11, ...	**(iii)**	A triangular number type sequence
	9	2, 6, 10, 14, 18, ...	**(i)**	A table-based sequence
	10	1, 6, 11, 16, 21, ...	**(i)**	A table-based sequence

(b) 1 $2n - 1$

2 n^2

3 $3n$

4 $\frac{1}{2}n(n + 1)$

5 $3n - 2$

6 $n^2 - 1$

7 A Fibonacci-style sequence

8 $\frac{1}{2}n(n - 1) + 1$

9 $4n - 2$

10 $5n - 4$

2 (a) 17, 20, 23; $3n - 1$

(b) 37, 50, 65; $n^2 + 1$

(c) 29, 37, 46; $\frac{1}{2}n(n + 1) + 1$

(d) 32, 37, 42; $5n - 3$

3 (a) $^-30, ^-35, ^-40; ^-5n$

(b) $^-18, ^-21, ^-24; ^-3n$

(c) $^-42, ^-49, ^-56; ^-7n$

(d) $^-24, ^-28, ^-32; ^-4n$

4 (a) $5, 0, ^-5; 35 - 5n$

(b) $^-6, ^-9, ^-12; 12 - 3n$

(c) 65, 58, 51; $107 - 7n$

(d) $0, ^-4, ^-8; 24 - 4n$

5 (a) $^-3, ^-6, ^-9; 18 - 3n$

(b) 33, 22, 11; $110 - 11n$

(c) 41, 39, 37; $53 - 2n$

(d) $^-7, ^-10, ^-13; 8 - 3n$

Exercise 8.3

1 (a) 32, 64, 128

(b) 0.5, 0.25, 0.125 or $\frac{1}{2}, \frac{1}{4}, \frac{1}{8}$

(c) 0.0625, 0.031 25, 0.015 625

(d) 0.01, 0.001, 0.0001

(e) 0.04, 0.008, 0.0016

2 (a) (i) 125, 216, 343

(ii) 625, 1296, 2401

(b) (i) n^3 (ii) n^4

3 (a) 5, 4, 6

(b) 7, 4, 9

(c) 7, 2, 9

(d) 16, 9, 32

4 (a) 5, 8, 11, 14, 17, 20

(b) 0, 3, 8, 15, 24, 35

(c) 4, 2, 1, 0.5, 0.25

(d) 2, 3, 5, 6, 8, 9, 11

(e) 2, 5, 7, 12, 19, 31

5 (a) 13, 17, 19, prime numbers

(b) F, S, S, days of the week

(c) A, S, O, months

(d) S, S, E, numbers

Exercise 8.4

1 (a) 3, 8, 23, 48 (b) 21st term is 103

2 (a) 9, 15, 21, 63 (b) 17th term is 105

3 (a) 17, 14, 11, $^{-}10$ (b) 7th term is $^{-}1$

4 (a) 4, 28, 103, 403 (b) 15th term is 228

5 (a) 2, 8, 18, 50 (b) 8th term is 128

6 (a) 98, 92, 68, $^{-}100$ (b) 8th term is $^{-}28$

7 (a) $^{-}1$, 0, 15, 80 (b) 12th term is 120

8 (a) 0, 4, 28, 108 (b) 14th term is 208

Exercise 8.5

1 (a)

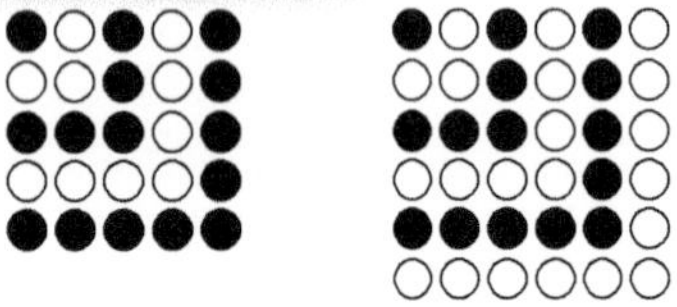

(b) If you have x^2 then you add $2x + 1$ to get the next square. As x increases, one by one, you generate the sequence of square numbers.

2 (a)

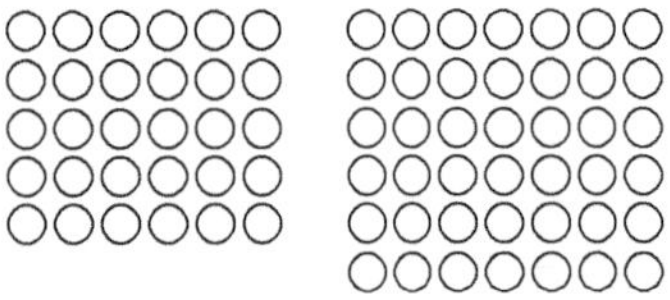

(b)

Rectangularnumber	Dots up	Dots along	Number of dots
1	1	2	$1 \times 2 = 2$
2	2	3	$2 \times 3 = 6$
3	3	4	$3 \times 4 = 12$
4	4	5	$4 \times 5 = 20$
5	5	6	$5 \times 6 = 30$
6	6	7	$6 \times 7 = 42$
n	n	$(n + 1)$	$n(n + 1)$

3 (a)

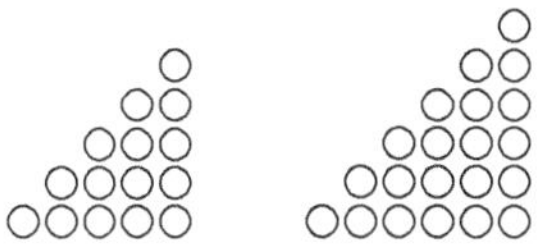

(b)

Pattern number	Triangular number
1	1
2	3
3	6
4	10
5	15
6	21

(c) Triangular numbers are half the rectangular numbers.

(d) $T_n = \frac{1}{2}n(n + 1)$

4 $n^2 - 1$

5 $n(n + 2)$

6 $\frac{1}{2}(n + 1)(n + 2) - 1$

7 $n(n + 1)$

Exercise 8.6

1 (a)

Patternnumber	White balls	Black balls	Total balls
1	1	0	1
2	2	2	4
3	5	4	9
4	8	8	16
5	13	12	25
6	18	18	36

(b) 100 (c) 50 (d) 50 (e) n^2

(f) If n is even, there will be $\frac{1}{2}n^2$ black balls and $\frac{1}{2}n^2$ white balls.

If n is odd, there will be $\frac{1}{2}(n^2 + 1)$ white balls and $\frac{1}{2}(n^2 - 1)$ black balls.

2 (a)

Pattern number	Black squares	White squares	Total squares
1	1	1	2
2	4	2	6
3	6	6	12
4	12	8	20
5	15	15	30
6	24	18	42

(b) 110 (c) 50 (d) 60

(e) If n is even, there will be $\frac{1}{2}n^2$ white squares and $\frac{1}{2}n(n+2)$ or $\frac{1}{2}n^2 + n$ black squares.

If n is odd, there will be $\frac{1}{2}n(n+1)$ black squares and $\frac{1}{2}n(n+1)$ white squares.

3 (a)

Pattern number	Black squares	White squares	Total squares
1	1	1	2
2	3	3	6
3	6	6	12
4	10	10	20
5	15	15	30
6	21	21	42

(b) 210 (c) 1275 (d) 10 100 (e) $\frac{1}{2}n(n+1)$

4 (a)

Pattern number	Black balls	White balls	Total balls
1	1	0	1
2	2	1	3
3	4	2	6
4	6	4	10
5	9	6	15
6	12	9	21

(b) 55 (c) 25 (d) 30 (e) $\frac{1}{2}n(n+1)$

(f) If n is even, there will be $\frac{1}{4}n^2$ black balls and $\frac{1}{4}n(n+2)$ white balls.

If n is odd, there will be $\frac{1}{4}(n+1)(n-1) = \frac{1}{4}n^2 - \frac{1}{4}$ black balls and $\frac{1}{4}(n+1)^2 = \frac{1}{4}n^2 + \frac{1}{2}n + \frac{1}{4}$ white balls.

5 (a)

Pattern number	Lines	Triangles
1	3	1
2	9	4
3	18	9
4	30	16
5	45	25
6	63	36

(b) 165 (c) 100 (d) 15 150

(e) $\frac{3}{2}n(n+1)$ (f) n^2

Extension Exercise 8.7

1 (a) Triangular numbers plus 1; $\frac{1}{2}n(n+1)+1$

(b) 3 × triangular numbers; $\frac{3}{2}n(n+1)$

(c) 2 × odd numbers; $2(2n-1)$ or $(4n-2)$

(d) 2 × triangle numbers − 1; $(n+1)(n+2)-2$ or (n^2+3n)

(e) Square numbers − 2; $(n+1)^2-2$

2 2, 6, 12, 20, 30; $n(n+1)$ or n^2+n

3 9, 25, 49, 81; $(2n+1)^2$

4 1, 4, 9, 16; n^2

5 2, 7, 15, 26, 40; $\frac{1}{2}n(3n+1)$

6 1, 2, 3, 4; n

Summary Exercise 8.8

1 (a) 22, 27, 32

(b) $\frac{1}{16}, \frac{1}{64}, \frac{1}{256}$

(c) $^-4, ^-6, ^-8$

2 (a) 13

(b) 31

(c) $3n+1$

3 (a)

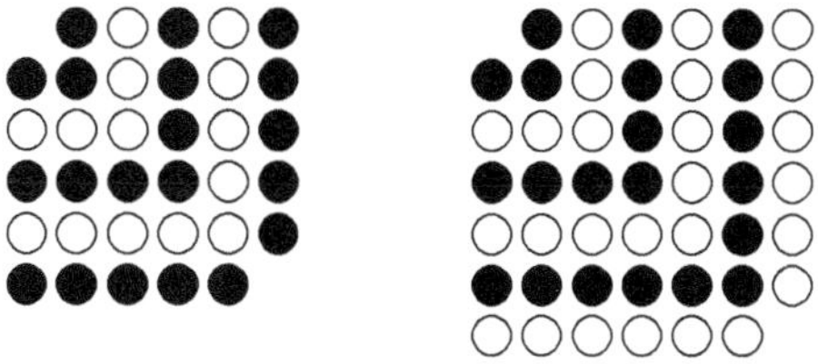

(b)

Pattern number	White balls	Red balls	Total balls
1	0	2	2
2	4	3	7
3	5	9	14
4	13	10	23
5	14	20	34
6	26	21	47

(c) If n is even: white balls = $\frac{1}{2}n(n+3) - 1$, red balls = $\frac{1}{2}n(n+1)$

If n is odd: white balls = $\frac{1}{2}(n-1)(n+2)$, red balls = $\frac{1}{2}n(n+3)$

Total number of balls = $(n+1)^2 - 2$

4 $S_1 = 17, S_4 = 8, S_6 = 2, S_{10} = {}^-10$

5 (a) 19, 22, 25; $3n + 1$

(b) 47, 62, 79; $(n + 1)^2 - 2$

(c) $^-5, {}^-7, {}^-9$; $7 - 2n$

6

1	1
1 + 1	2
1 + 2 + 1	4
1 + 3 + 3 + 1	8
1 + 4 + 6 + 4 + 1	16

(a) 2^{n-1}

(b) Third diagonal

(c) 1, 4, 10, 20, 35, they increase by triangular numbers or are the sum of triangular numbers.

(d) The sum of n triangular numbers.

7 (a) (i) 8

(ii) 13

(iii) 21

(b) 144

Activity: An introduction to fractals

Fractals are fascinating but the mathematics behind them very quickly runs into very complicated sequences. The one chosen here is accessible to pupils at this level. It gives a clear example of a geometric design that leads to a numerical sequence that in turn can be described by an algebraic rule. Those pupils who are not inspired by algebra frequently enjoy the progression of the patterns.

1 (a)

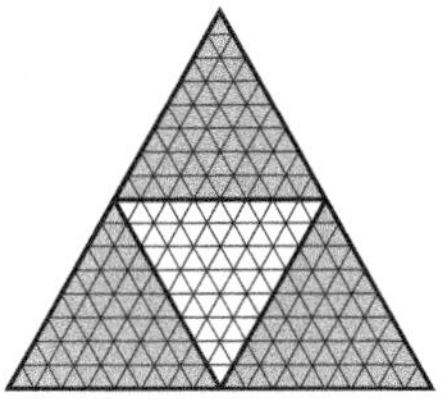

(b)

(c)

(d)

Generation number	1	2	3	4	5
Number of triangles (including the unshaded ones)	4	13	40	121	364
Fraction of whole	$\frac{1}{4}$	$\frac{7}{16}$	$\frac{37}{64}$	$\frac{175}{256}$	$\frac{781}{1024}$

(e) The number of triangles (including the unshaded ones) in the nth generation can be expressed as $\frac{(3^{n+1}-1)}{2}$

2 (a)

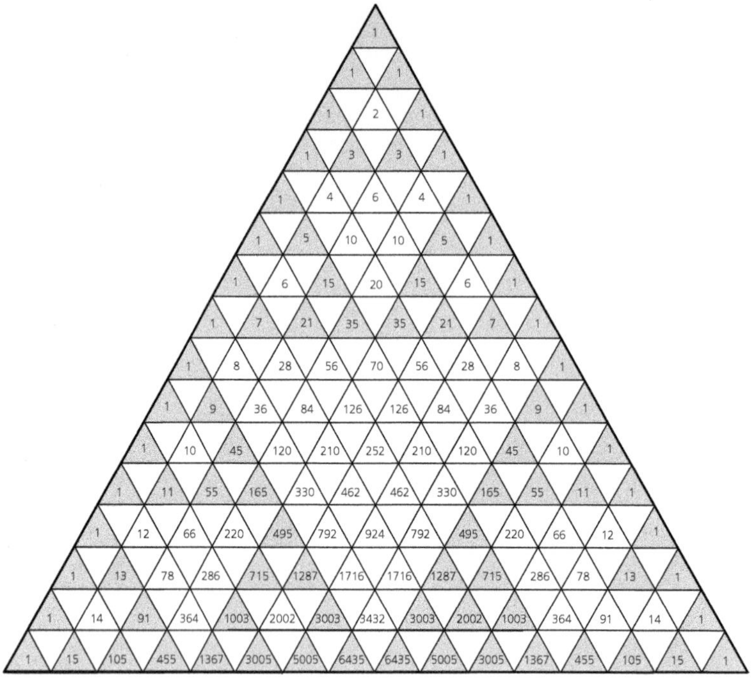

(b) See diagram above.

(c) The pattern is the same! Amazing isn't it? The explanation could be given as follows, where E is an even number and O is odd.

										O											
									O		O										
								O		E		O									
							O		O		O		O								
						O		E		E		E		O							
					O		O		E		E		O		O						
				O		E		O		E		O		E		O					
			O		O		O		O		O		O		O		O				

Pupils may also enjoy the Koch Snowflake.

9 Using formulae

Exercise 9.1

1 $N = x + y$

2 $N = a - b$

3 $A = \frac{w+x+y+z}{4}$

4 $P = 14x + 6$

5 $A = 3x(4x + 3)$

6 $P = 6x + 2$

7 $A = x(x + 4)$

8 $N = 100(x + y)$

9 $N = \frac{x+y}{100}$

10 $N = 10y$

11 $N = ny$

12 $N = \frac{nx}{100}$

13 $P = 6a + 6b$

14 $A = 5ab$

15 $P = 10a + 6b$

16 $A = 9ab$

17 $A = x^2 - y^2$

18 $A = xy - (x - 10)(y - 10)$ which simplifies to $A = 10(x + y - 10)$

Exercise 9.2

1 (a) $N = {}^-3$ (b) $N = 2$ (c) $N = {}^-1$ (d) $N = {}^-8$ (e) $N = 1$ (f) $N = {}^-4$

2 (a) $N = 9$ (b) $N = 2$ (c) $N = 13$ (d) $N = {}^-18$ (e) $N = {}^-5$ (f) $N = 144$

3 (a) $N = 0.1$ (b) $N = 0.6$ (c) $N = 1.04$ (d) $N = {}^-3$ (e) $N = {}^-0.2$ (f) $N = {}^-7.92$

4 (a) $M = {}^-0.75$ or $-\frac{3}{4}$ (b) $M = 0.2$ or $\frac{1}{5}$ (c) $M = 12$ (d) $M = 8$ (e) $M = 3$ (f) $M = \frac{25}{14}$

5 (a) $N = {}^-4$ (b) $N = 8$ (c) $N = 4$ (d) $N = {}^-14$ (e) $N = 6$ (f) $N = 70$

6 (a) $N = 1.0584$ (d) $N = {}^{-}1.20204$

(b) $N = {}^{-}0.126$ (e) $N = 0.1512$

(c) $N = 0.254016$ (f) $N = 0.9834048$

7 (a) $N = {}^{-}12$ (d) $N = {}^{-}3$

(b) $N = {}^{-}4.5$ or ${}^{-}4\frac{1}{2}$ (e) $N = 12$

(c) $N = 36$ (f) $N = {}^{-}20$

8 (a) $A = 9.6149$ (d) $A = {}^{-}160$

(b) $A = {}^{-}0.444875$ (e) $A = 9.5225$

(c) $A = {}^{-}4.092$ (f) $A = 0.54$

9 (a) $V = 0.625$ (d) $N = {}^{-}8.525$

(b) $N = {}^{-}1.369$ (e) $V = 7.75$

(c) $V = {}^{-}3.845$

10 (a) $N = {}^{-}2.4465$ (d) $N = 0.3625$

(b) $N = 21.7375$ (e) $N = 1.9$

(c) $N = 1.334025$

Area and volume formulae

This next exercise provides a good opportunity to revise all those formulae that the pupils should know at this stage. Do insist that the pupils set out their answers correctly right from the start.

Exercise 9.3

1 $7.84\,cm^2$

2 $3.7\,m$

3 $1.728\,m^3$

4 $0.715\,m^2$

5 $1.053\,m^3$

6 594 litres

7 $0.63375\,m^2$

8 Area of a kite $= \frac{ab}{2}$, area $= 90\,cm^2$

9 Surface area of a cube $= 6x^2$, surface area $= 864\,cm^2$

10 Surface area of a cuboid $= 2wl + 2wh + 2lh = 2(wl + wh + lh)$; surface area $= 1376\,cm^2$

Finding an unknown quantity

If these questions are solved in the way equations are solved they will become simple.

Exercise 9.4

1 17 cm
2 19 cm
3 17 cm
4 48 cm
5 7 cm
6 12 cm
7 4.57 m
8 1.6 cm and 3.2 cm
9 24 cm
10 3.6 m
11 Base 3.87 cm
12 12.2 cm
13 8.66 cm and 11.55 cm
14 13.4 cm and 22.4 cm

Distance, speed and time formulae

The fraction button of the calculator can be helpful in this exercise.

Exercise 9.5

1 45 miles
2 1 hour 30 minutes
3 2.25 mph
4 30 000 mph
5 2500 km
6 40 miles
7 90 km/h
8 2 hours 32 minutes
9 618 mph
10 Average daily distance = 522 km, speed = 21.75 knots
11 Twice as long
12 It travels 3 times as fast.
13 It travels 6 times as fast.

Exercise 9.6

1 (a) 41.25 km (b) 55 km/h
2 (a) $1\frac{5}{6}$ km (b) 4.4 km/h
3 (a) 220 km (b) 110 km/h
4 (a) 1250 km (b) 312.5 km/h
5 67 mph
6 90 km/h
7 (a) 227 km/h (b) 2 hours 12 minutes

Units of formulae

This is omitted from the Common Entrance syllabus but it is a useful exercise to ensure that pupils do understand how to check their formulae and calculations.

Exercise 9.7

1 (a) metres, distance (b) seconds, time

2 (a) g/cm^3, density (b) cm^3, volume

3 (a) area (b) length (c) length (d) volume (e) length (f) volume (g) area

4 (a) g/m^3 (b) m (c) seconds

Extension Exercise 9.8

1 $x = y - 3$

2 $x = y + 5$

3 $x = y - a$

4 $x = y + b$

5 $x = d - y$

6 $x = \frac{y}{2}$

7 $x = \frac{y}{a}$

8 $x = 2y$

9 $x = by$

10 $x = \frac{y-3}{2}$

11 $x = \frac{y+4}{3}$

12 $x = \frac{y+b}{2}$

13 $x = \frac{y-c}{3}$

14 $x = \frac{y-b}{a}$

15 $x = \frac{y+d}{c}$

16 $x = \frac{y}{a} + b$

17 $x = \frac{ay}{3}$

18 $x = \frac{by}{a}$

19 $x = \frac{2a}{y}$

20 $x = \frac{3b}{2y}$

21 $x = cy - b$

22 $x = \frac{3y}{2} + 1$

23 $x = \frac{cy}{a} + b$

24 $x = \frac{ab}{y} + 1$

25 $x = 2(y - 1)$

26 $x = \frac{y+5}{a}$

27 $x = \frac{ay}{2} - ab$

28 $x = \frac{2a}{y}$

29 $x = \frac{ab}{y} + c$

30 $x = \frac{b(a+d)}{y} + c$

Summary Exercise 9.9

1 $P = 8a + 12b$

2 $A = 12ab$

3 (a) $N = {}^{-}3$ (c) $N = 8$ (e) $N = 15$

(b) $N = \frac{^{-}1}{4}$ (d) $N = 1\frac{1}{2}$ (f) $N = {}^{-}12$

4 32 cm

5 (a) 1.14 cm^2 (b) 2.67 cm

6 6.17 cm

7 12.5 hours

8 (a) $56\frac{2}{3}$ km/h (b) $56\frac{2}{3}$ km

9 (a) $x = a - y$

(b) $x = \frac{y-c}{a}$

(c) $x = \frac{ha-by}{h}$

10 (a) (i) 10 miles (ii) 1 hour (iii) 40 mph

(b) No. He spent 40 minutes in town and that left him 20 minutes on the motorway. He must have travelled at 90 mph.

Activity: The cube root trick

A remarkable fact about cubes is that when you look at their last digits there are no duplicates. If the cube ends with 1, then the cube root ends with 1. If the last digit ends with 2 then the cube root ends with 8. It is worth exploring this with your pupils before they try the 'trick'.

Last digit cube	Last digit cube root
1	1
2	8
3	7
4	4
5	5
6	6
7	3
8	2
9	9
0	0

10 Geometry

There is little new content in this chapter but the questions are more complex than those in Mathematics for Common Entrance *Book 2, hence no extension exercise.*

Exercise 10.1

1 (a) 135° (b) $202\frac{1}{2}°$ (c) $067\frac{1}{2}°$ (d) $337\frac{1}{2}°$

2 (a) south-west (c) south-south-east
(b) north-north-east (d) west-north-west

3 (a) 225° (b) 020° (c) 298° (d) 132°

4 (a) $\angle ABC = 40°$ (angles in a triangle add up to 180°)
(b) The bearing of C from A = 042° (112° − 70°)
(c) The bearing of C from B = 332° (180° + 112° + 40°)

5 (a) 044° (b) 102°

6 (a) 235° (b) 055°

7 (a)

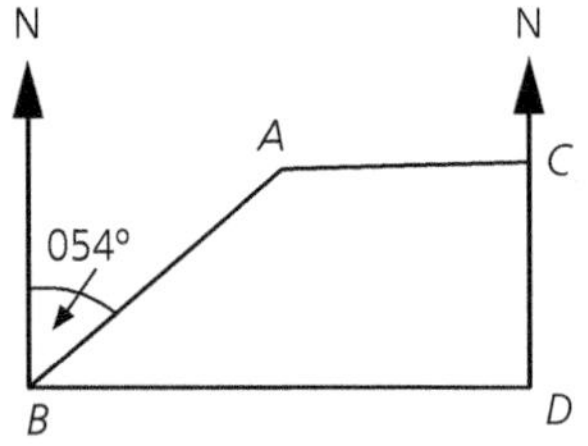

(b) $\angle BAD = 99°$

8 (a)

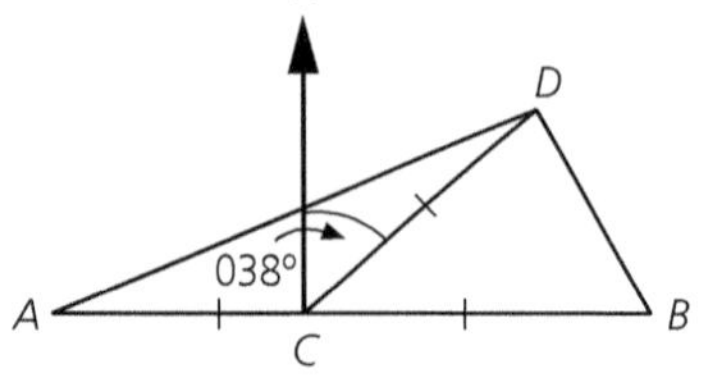

(b) 154° (c) 244°

Polygon formulae

This exercise provides a good opportunity to revise formulae associated with polygons as well as angle facts. Make sure that pupils understand the distinction between regular and irregular polygons.

Exercise 10.2

1 540°	4 60°	7 120°	10 15
2 1260°	5 51.4°	8 135°	11 12
3 1080°	6 36°	9 20	12 18

Exercise 10.3

You may wish to revise properties of quadrilaterals before starting this exercise.

1 (a) $\angle AOB = 72°$ (b) $\angle OBC = 54°$ (c) $\angle ABC = 108°$

2 (a) $\angle CDG = 60°$ (b) $\angle CDE = 120°$ (c) $\angle DCF = 60°$ (d) They are parallel.

3 (a) $\angle BAF = 120°$ (b) $\angle ECD = 30°$ (c) It is a rectangle, all angles are 90°

4 (a) $\angle BAH = 135°$ (b) $\angle HBA = 22.5°$ (c) $\angle HBC = 112.5°$ (d) It is a trapezium.

(e) It is a parallelogram, *BH* is parallel to *CX* and *BC* is parallel to *HX*.

5 (a) $\angle EOF = 45°$ (b) $\angle FED = 135°$ (c) $\angle OED = 67.5°$ (d) $\angle BCD = 135°$ (e) $\angle CDB = 22.5°$ (f) $\angle BDE = 112.5°$ (g) They are parallel as $\angle BDE + \angle OED = 180°$

6 (a) $\angle CDE = 108°$ (b) $\angle EDF = 120°$ (c) $\angle CED = 36°$ (d) $\angle DEF = 30°$ (e) $\angle CDF = 132°$ (obtuse) or 228° (reflex) (f) $\angle ECF = 60°$

7 24

8 Pupils may give other valid reasons.

(a) (i) $\angle GHA = 135°$, interior angle of regular octagon

(ii) $\angle HGB = 45°$, corresponding angles, interior angles in parallel lines

(iii) $\angle GOF = 45°$, angles at a point

(iv) $\angle FGE = (180° - 135°) \div 2 = 22.5°$, base angle of isosceles triangle

(v) $x = 90°$ (180° – (67.5° + 22.5°), angles in a triangle

(vi) $y = 45°$ (67.5° – 22.5°)

(b) Kite, 2 pairs of adjacent equal sides.

9 Pupils may give other valid reasons.

(a) 9 sides

(b) (i) 40°, angles at a point

(ii) 40°, corresponding angles

(iii) 70°, base angles of isosceles triangle

(iv) 30°, base angles of isosceles triangle

10 Pupils may give other valid reasons.

(i) $\angle BCD = 156°$, interior angle of 15-sided polygon

(ii) $\angle CBE = 24°$, corresponding angles, interior angles in parallel lines

(iii) $\angle FEB = 132°$ (156° – 24°)

(iv) $\angle BAF = 48°$, co-interior angles

(v) $\angle DCE = 12°$, base angle of isosceles triangle

(vi) $\angle AFB = 12°$, corresponding angles with $FBE = BEC = DCE$

Exercise 10.4

You can use the sine and cosine rules to calculate dimensions in these constructions and astonish your pupils.

Exact answers may vary due to pupils' own measurements.

1 (a), (b) Check pupils' constructions.

(c) $CD = 5.4$ cm

(d) 21.6 cm^2

2 (a) (b) Check pupils' constructions.

(c) $FX = 6.5$ cm

(d) 29.25 cm^2

3 (a) (b) Check pupils' constructions.

(c) $RX = 4.6$ cm

(d) 17.25 cm^2

Exercise 10.5

The purpose of this exercise is not simply to give practice with construction but also to make pupils think about the properties of the shapes they create.

1 **(a)–(d)** Check pupils' constructions.

(e) Rhombus. All sides are equal. Two pairs of parallel sides. Two pairs of equal angles. Diagonals bisect each other at right angles. Diagonals bisect the angles. Two lines of symmetry. Rotational symmetry of order 2

2 **(a)–(d)** Check pupils' constructions.

(e) Kite. Two pairs of equal sides. One pair of equal angles. One diagonal bisects the other at right angles. One diagonal bisects the non-equal angles and is a line of symmetry.

3 **(a)–(d)** Check pupils' constructions.

(e) Isosceles arrowhead. Two pairs of equal sides. One pair of equal angles. One diagonal bisects the other at right angles. One diagonal bisects the non-equal angles and is a line of symmetry.

4 **(a)–(b)** Check pupils' constructions.

(c) At *E*

(d) It is a line of symmetry.

5 **(a)–(d)** Check pupils' constructions.

6 Check pupils' constructions.

Summary Exercise 10.6

1 201°

2 $x = 180° - 96° - 54° = 30°$

3 144°

4 16 sides

5 Other reasons may be valid.

(a) $x = 135°$, interior angle of regular octagon

$\angle GOD = 3 \times \frac{360°}{8} = 135°$, angles at centre

$w = \frac{180° - 135°}{2} = 22.5°$, base angle of isosceles triangle

$y = 180° - 135° = 45°$, co-interior angles

$z = 360° - (225° - 22.5° - 22.5°) = 90°$, angle sum of quadrilateral *OGPD*

(b) Right-angled trapezium. Two right angles, one pair of lines parallel

6 **(a)–(b)** Check pupils' constructions.

(c) $CD = 6.3\text{ cm}$, area $= 28.35\text{ cm}^2$. Answers may vary due to pupil's measurements.

Activity: Perigal's dissection

They should all fit together like this.

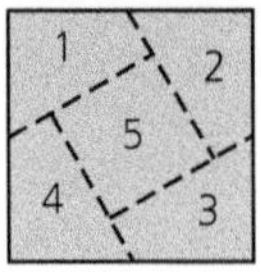

This is not strictly a 'proof' of Pythagoras' theorem but it will probably convince your class. Until they can expand brackets, they do not have the mathematics to comprehend a formal proof.

If they can expand brackets, then the following is probably the simplest (I am indebted to Giles Kirby for this one).

Consider a square of side c (see diagram) inscribed inside a square of side $(a + b)$

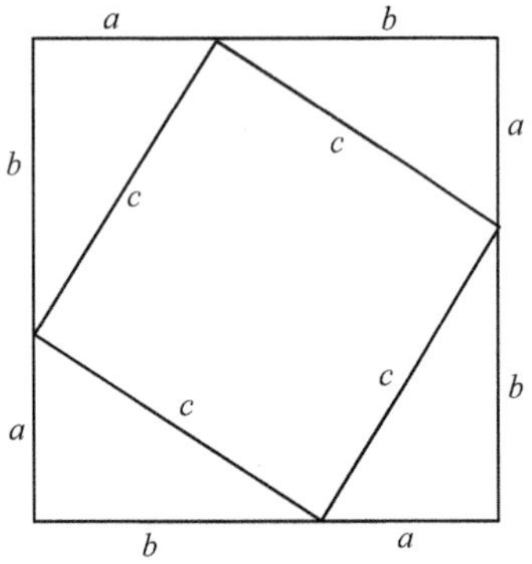

The area of the large square is:

$(a + b)^2 = a^2 + 2ab + b^2$

Also the area of the large square = area of small square + area of 4 triangles

$$= c^2 + 4 \times \frac{1}{2}ab$$
$$= c^2 + 2ab$$

Therefore:

$$a^2 + 2ab + b^2 = c^2 + 2ab \qquad (-\,2ab)$$
$$a^2 + b^2 = c^2$$

Therefore in the right-angled triangle with sides a, b and c the square of the hypotenuse is equal to the sum of the squares of the other two sides!

11 Pythagoras' theorem

This introduction to Pythagoras' theorem is also an introduction to the elements of trigonometry. Pupils should be encouraged to get into the habit of making a neat clear sketch, identifying and labelling the hypotenuse before they do anything else.

Exercise 11.1

1

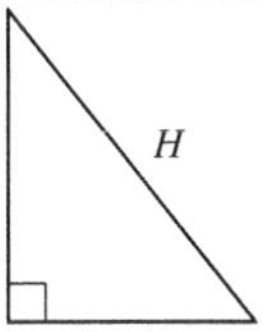

2

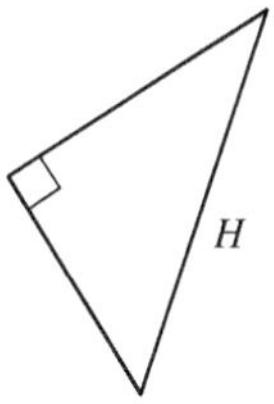

3

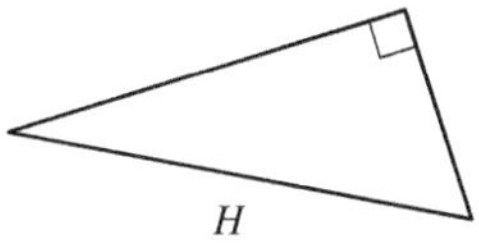

4

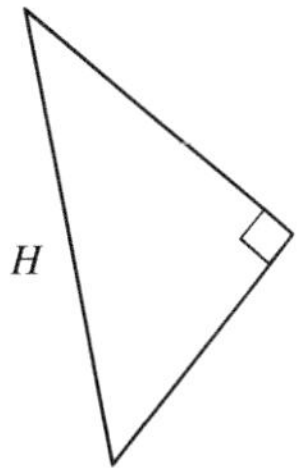

5

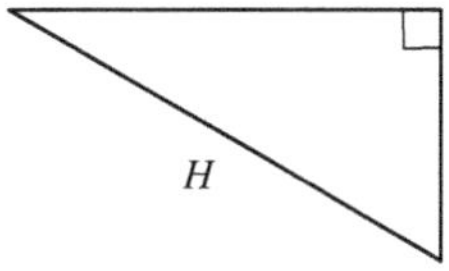

6

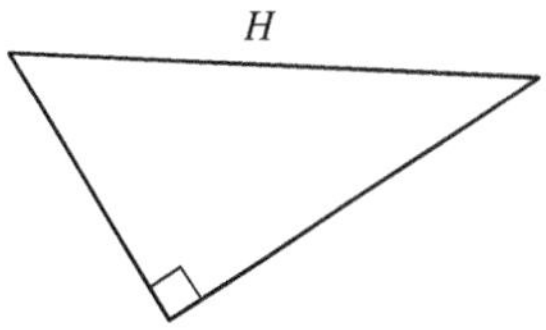

Exercise 11.2

1 5 cm

2 7.21 cm

3 10.77 cm

4 9.22 m

5 3 km

6 2.20 cm

7 13 cm

8 2.6 cm

9 11.31 mm

Exercise 11.3

1 10 miles

2 400 km

3 3.04 km (∠*ABC* is 90°)

4 John runs 300 m and Janet runs 335 m so Janet runs further.

5 7.07 cm

6 No, diagonal is 2.236 m. I must shave 6.4 cm off first.

7 (a) 5.02 m

(b) No, the ladder would reach only 39 cm up the wall. The ladder would need to be 5.32 m long.

Exercise 11.4

1 12 cm

2 1.59 m

3 40 m

4 17.35 m

5 80 m

6 1.5 km

7 11.18 cm

8 150 m

9 5.29 m

Exercise 11.5

1 9.95 cm

2 25.98 miles

3 1.87 km

4 3.87 m

5 2.24 m

6 0.97 m

7 3.54 cm

8 5.37 cm and 10.73 cm

By now your quicker pupils may want to write out the formula in an abbreviated form. Certainly going straight to the square root can be faster to write down but it can lead to careless mistakes. Potential scholars will benefit from the opportunity to work in roots. For others perhaps the discipline of the stage by stage working is still the safest.

Isosceles triangles

Pupils often make mistakes in this exercise. Commonly they forget to halve the base and forget to subtract the squares.

Exercise 11.6

1 7.19 cm

2 5.20 cm

3 1.32 m

4 10 cm

5 9.24 cm

Special triangles

Being able to spot special triangles is essential for those taking scholarship papers. Many papers are non-calculator which can be a bit of a giveaway that a special triangle is being used.

Exercise 11.7

1 $3:4:5\ \Delta \times 0.3, x = 0.9$

2 Not a special triangle, $x = 3.54$

3 $3:4:5\ \Delta \times 60, x = 240$

4 $5:12:13\ \Delta \times 5, x = 65$

5 Not a special triangle, $x = 3.20$

6 $3:4:5\ \Delta \times 70, x = 210$

7 $5:12:13\ \Delta \times 5, x = 195$

8 Not a special triangle, $x = 66.14$

Exercise 11.8

1. 2.5 m

2 9 m

3 (a) 12 m

(b) 13 m

4 1300 m

5 1000 m or 1 km

6 250 m

7 12 m

Extension Exercise 11.9

1 $PQ = 5.29$ cm, $RS = 4.77$ cm

2 28.3 cm and 44.7 cm

3 $CD = 4.58$ cm and $BD = 11.1$ cm

4 (a) No!

(b) 29 cm, so it is 1.71 m from the wall.

5 (a) $CD = 7.07$ cm

(b) $CF = 3.54$ cm

(c) $EF = 5$ cm

(d) $CG = 2.5$ cm

6 17.2 cm, there are two different ways of drawing the spider's route on the net.

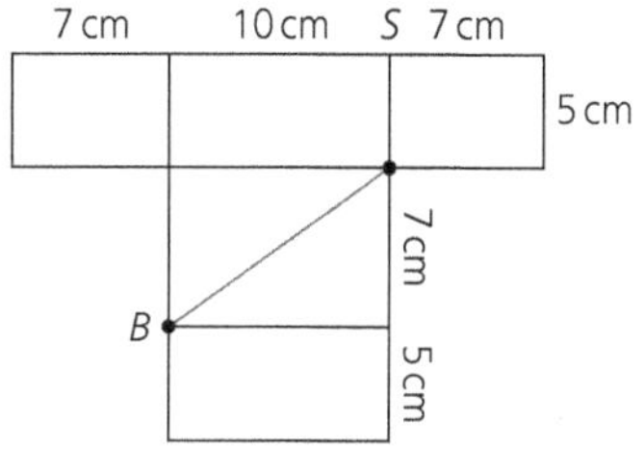

7 (a) $AB = 3.16$ or $\sqrt{10}$, $AC = 6.08$ or $\sqrt{37}$ and $BC = 5.39$ or $\sqrt{29}$

(b) No, the square on the longest side is not the sum of the squares on the other two sides.

8 6.25 km

Ella worked out that they had turned through a right angle and had walked two sides of a 3 : 4 : 5 triangle (× 1.25).

9 (a) $AC = 17.0$ cm

(b) $FC = 13.4$ cm

(c) The areas of triangles: $AFB = 36\,\text{cm}^2$; $BCF = 72\,\text{cm}^2$; $AFC = 36\,\text{cm}^2$

(d) Calculate angles and you will find that triangles GBC and AGF are similar.

Area of triangle $GBC = 48\,\text{cm}^2$ and triangle $AGF = 12\,\text{cm}^2$

10 As in the last question, triangles AGB and FGC are similar. You can therefore find the height and thus the area of triangle ABG. Area of triangle BCG = area of rectangle less the area of triangles ADC and ABG. It is a little unnerving to find a Pythagoras question ending with similar triangles but this is what scholars should expect.

Area of triangle $GBA = 16\,\text{cm}^2$ and triangle $GBC = 32\,\text{cm}^2$

Summary Exercise 11.10

1 For any right-angled triangle the square on the hypotenuse is equal to the sum of the squares on the other two sides.

2 4.72 km

3 Height = 60.9 cm and area = $975\,\text{cm}^2$

4 (a) The length $AD = 6.08$ m

(b) $7.90\,\text{m}^2$

(c) The length $AE = 2$ m and length $AB = 1.52$ m

(d) Area $BCFE = 3.95\,\text{m}^2$

5 $BE = 1.86$ m

6 (a) $AD = 5.83$ cm

(b) Area ABC is $2.7\,\text{cm}^2$ and area CDE is $1.2\,\text{cm}^2$

Activity: Pythagorean triplets

When looking at these triplets it can be interesting to make up a table to show the last digits of the squares and their sums.

Square numbers only end in the digits: 0, 1, 4, 5, 6, 9, and thus the possible sums are:

	0	1	4	5	6	9
0	0	1	4	5	6	9
1	1	2	5	6	7	0
4	4	5	8	9	3	3
5	5	6	9	0	1	4
6	6	7	0	4	2	5
9	9	0	3	4	5	8

The squares of multiples of 5 end in 0 or 5

If you look at the table, you will see that in one out of three results, for the sum of two squares is a multiple of 5

That should help the search.

There are hundreds of Pythagorean triplets to find and because there is so much information available on the internet this activity should remain in the classroom (preferably one without access to a computer).

Here are a few Pythagorean triplets, note multiples of 5

3 : 4 : 5	8 : 6 : 10	15 : 8 : 17	12 : 16 : 20
5 : 12 : 13	24 : 10 : 26	21 : 20 : 29	16 : 30 : 34
7 : 24 : 25	35 :12 : 37	32 : 24 : 40	27 : 36 : 45
9 : 40 : 41	20 : 48 : 52	48 : 14 : 50	45 : 28 : 53
11 : 60 : 61	40 : 42 : 58	33 : 56 : 65	24 : 70 : 74

12 Circles, cylinders and prisms

Circles

The most common mistakes pupils make is to confuse the formulae for area and volume and to substitute the radius instead of the diameter. It is therefore good discipline to insist that they draw the circle and mark the given length first. They can then do the calculation.

Exercise 12.1

1 (i) The circumference

(a) 25.1 cm (c) 3.77 m (e) 157 cm

(b) 195 cm (d) 28.3 m (f) 75.4 m

(ii) The area

(a) 50.3 cm^2 (c) 1.13 m^2 (e) 1960 cm^2

(b) 3020 cm^2 (d) 63.6 m^2 (f) 452 m^2

2 2.98 m

3 Area = 154 cm^2, circumference = 44.0 cm

4 50.3 cm^2

5 56.5 cm

6. 1.90 m^2

Exercise 12.2

1 231 cm

2 Area = 154 cm^2 and perimeter = 50.0 cm

3 1470 cm^2

4 (a) 206 m (b) 2860 m^2

5 283 cm^2

6 (a) 43.6 cm^2 28.7 cm

(b) 2410 mm^2 207 mm

7 193 m^2

8 4.7 m

9 4720 mm^2

10 (a) 88 cm (b) 504 cm^2 (c) 280 cm^2

Exercise 12.3

1 4.46 cm

2 5.64 cm

3 1.91 m

4 17.8 cm

5 113 cm

6 31.8 cm

7 1.26 m

8 7.78 cm

Exercise 12.4

1 (a) 10 cm (b) 14.1 cm

2 14.1 cm, 156 cm^2

3 56.1 cm^2 (Remind the pupils not to work with rounded answers!)

4 (a) 15.6 cm (b) 68.4 cm^2

5 98 cm^2

6 576 cm^2

7 35.4 cm

8 (a) $\frac{\pi x^2}{2}$ (b) $2x^2$ (c) $2\pi x^2$ (d) $4x^2$

9 (a) 3.46 cm

(b) 6.93 cm^2

(c) 12.6 cm^2

(d) 2.09 cm^2

(e) 9.52%

10 20, 21.5%

Exercise 12.5

Practical activity

Exercise 12.6

1 (a) $3.5\,m^3$ (b) $96\,cm^3$ (c) $72\,m^3$ (d) $224\,m^3$

2 $67.5\,cm^3$

3 $1000\,cm^3$

4 Volume = $297\,cm^3$

5 $1.596\,m^3$

6 $8.64\,m^3$

7 (a) The square cross-section

(b) The triangular section and rectangular section would overflow and the square section would be just full.

8 $4320\,cm^3$

9 $8\,cm^2$

10 (a) $6.28\,m^2$ (b) 314

Exercise 12.7

1 (a) (i) $141\,cm^3$ (ii) 0.141 litres

(b) (i) $251\,000\,000\,cm^3$ (ii) 251 000 litres

(c) (i) $141\,000\,cm^3$ (ii) 141 litres

(d) (i) $5090\,cm^3$ (ii) 5.09 litres

(e) (i) $1410\,cm^3$ (ii) 1.41 litres

(f) (i) $2\,120\,000\,cm^3$ (ii) 2120 litres

2 $4.83\,m^3$

3 1140 litres

4 8

5 $942\,cm^3$

Exercise 12.8

1 12 cm high and 31.4 cm along, area = $377\,cm^2$

2 (a) $314\,cm^2$ (b) $785\,cm^3$

3 $4320\,cm^2$

4 (a) $150\,cm^2$ (b) To give it strength

5 $683\,cm^2$

6 Cube by 129 cm^2

7 The one with radius of 6 cm and a height 5 cm is larger by 30π.

8 22.6 litres

9 47 bucket loads

10 15.0 cm

Exercise 12.9

1 (a) 100
(b) 1 000 000
(c) 1 000 000
(d) 0.0001
(e) 0.000 001
(f) 0.000 001

2 (a) 1000
(b) 1 000 000 000
(c) 1 000 000 000
(d) 0.000 001
(e) 0.000 000 001
(f) 0.000 000 001

3 (a) 1000
(b) 1 000 000

Extension Exercise 12.10

1 18 cm

2 1.27 m

3 2 cm

4 19.4 cm

5 10.6 cm

6 4 litres

7 (a) 5620 cm^3
(b) 3380 cm^2

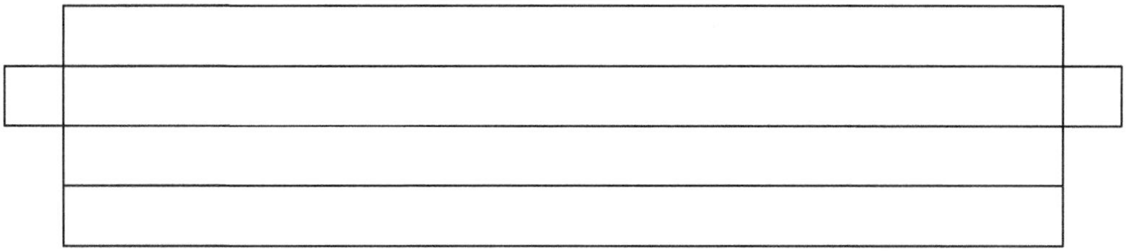

8 51.7 cm

9 (a) 283 cm^3
(b) 2160 cm^3
(c) 21.5%

10 (a) 4520 cm^3 (b) 25 cm

Remember to add the 0.5 to the top, not to the sides.

(c) 10 cm by 78.5 cm

This assumes you take 25 cm for the diameter – if you take 24 cm it would be too small.

(d) 630 cm^3 (e) 573 cm^3

You may need to explain how to make icing but if you have got this far a sugary interlude would probably be enjoyed by all.

Summary Exercise 12.11

1 Area = 1.33 m^2; circumference = 4.08 m

2 Area = 2.05 m^2 and perimeter = 5.73 m

3 3.41 times

4 1800 cm^3

5 4.37 cm

6 (a) 6.17 cm (b) 9 cm

7 11.05 cm

8 (a) 3 054 000 litres (b) 4.14 m (c) 18.47 m

9 (a) 12 cm by 38.7 cm (b) 21

In these problems about labels you cannot divide the area of the big sheet by the area of the label, you have to see how many labels will go along each side, in this case 7 by 3 is 21 labels.

10 (a) 123 cm^2 (b) 92.0 cm^2 (c) 401 cm^2 (d) 64.2%

Activity: Packaging the litre

This is an excellent opportunity to do some cross-curricular work with Art or Design technology. Gather together as many examples of litre containers as you can. Discuss their merits, not only in appearance but how they would stack on a shelf, be packaged in a box, or how their net is constructed. You can investigate various nets and introduce pupils to other volume formulae beyond CE and CASE, for example:

Cube	side^3
Rectangular Prism	side1 × side2 × side3
Sphere	$\left(\frac{4}{3}\right)$ × pi × radius^3
Cylinder	pi × radius^2 × height
Cone	$\left(\frac{1}{3}\right)$ × pi × radius^2 × height
Pyramid	$\left(\frac{1}{3}\right)$ × (base area) × height

13 Simultaneous equations

In this chapter pupils will start to pull together the skills of simplifying, solving and substituting. If you have not revised these techniques first then it would be good to do so. You may also wish to go through scaling up an equation as well as simplifying expressions.

The purely abstract idea of solving the equation by elimination is alien to many pupils of this age, therefore this chapter explores the relationship between equations and graphs first.

Exercise 13.1

1 $x + y = 24$

2 $x - y = 8$

3 $2x + y = 20$

4 $x + y = 15$

5 $25x + 30y = 300$

These last two questions are typical of the types of equation set at this level. Make sure pupils understand that in question 4 you are looking at total number and in question 5 total price. Pupils will meet more of this in the later exercises.

Exercise 13.2

1 (a)

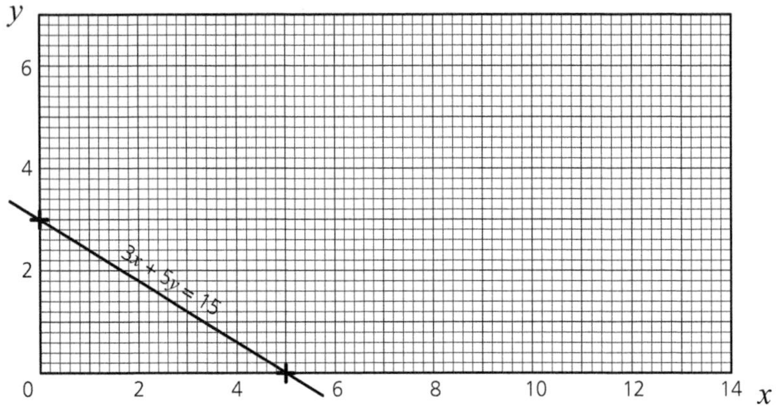

(b)

x	y
0	3
5	0

2 (a)

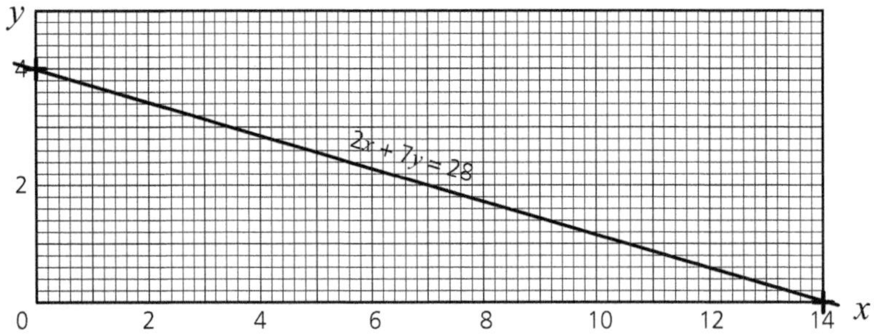

(b)

x	y
0	4
7	2
14	0

3

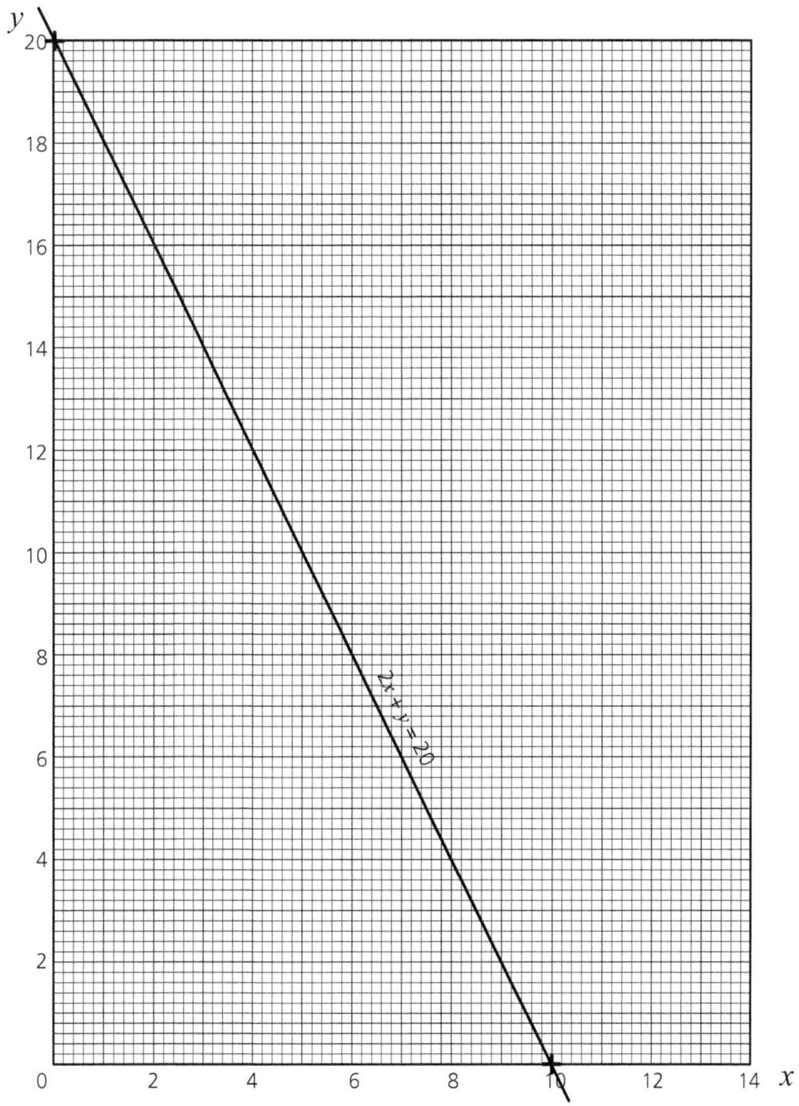

Numbers I could be thinking of:

x	0	1	2	3	4	5	6	7	8	9	10
y	20	18	16	14	12	10	8	6	4	2	0

4

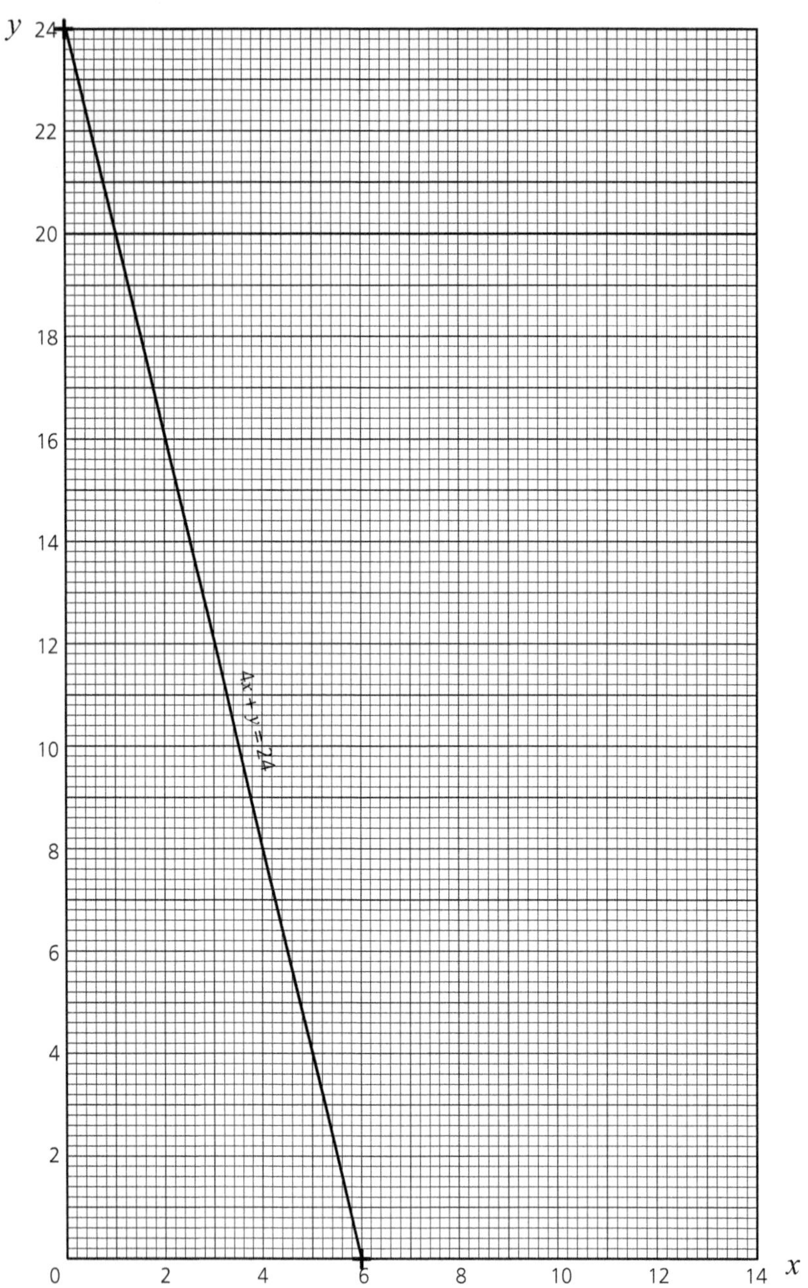

Numbers I could be thinking of:

x	0	1	2	3	4	5	6
y	24	20	16	12	8	4	0

5 (a) $80m + 160j = 800 \rightarrow (\div 80) \rightarrow m + 2j = 10$

(b)

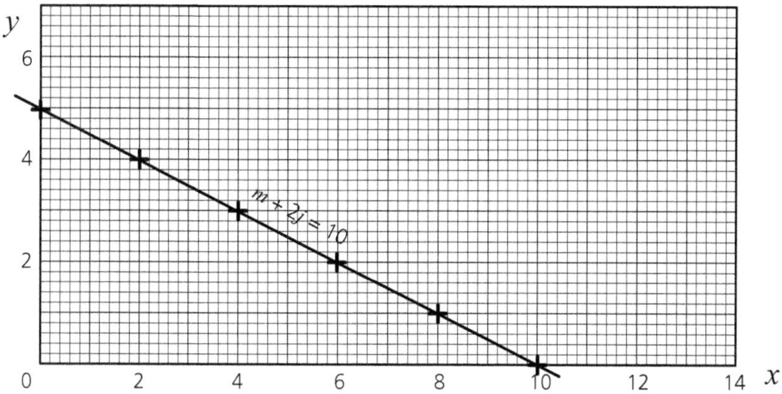

Litres of milk and juice

m	0	2	4	6	8	10
j	5	4	3	2	1	0

(c) 2 litres of milk and 4 litres of juice

6 (a) $450x + 150y = 1350 \rightarrow (\div 150) \rightarrow 3x + y = 9$

(b)

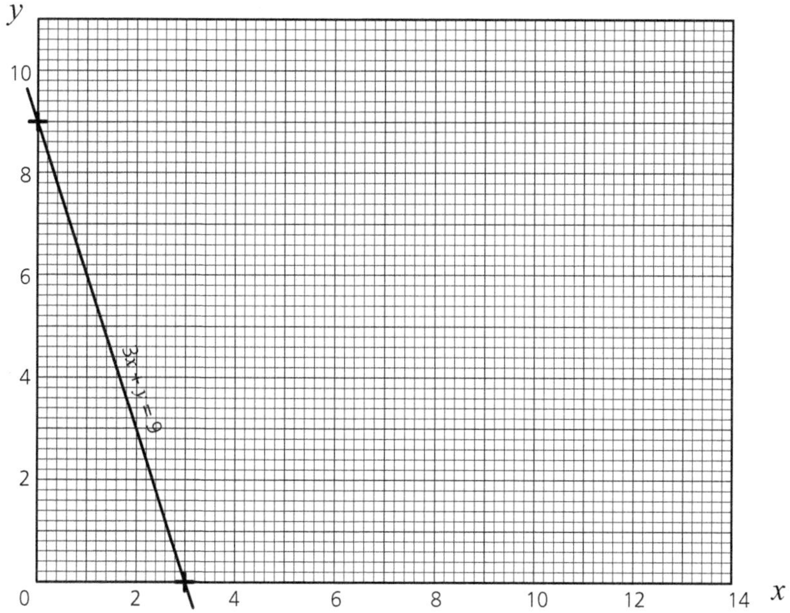

(c)

x	Batteries	y	Batteries
0	0	9	27
1	5	6	18
2	10	3	9
3	15	0	0

(d) 2 packs of long life and 3 packs of ordinary batteries

Exercise 13.3

1 (a) $x = 7, y = 7$
(b) $x = 14, y = 0$
(c) $x = 2, y = 2$
(d) $x = 12, y = 2$
(e) $x = 0, y = 8$
(f) $x = 4\frac{1}{2}, y = 9\frac{1}{2}$
(g) $x = 3\frac{3}{7}, y = 6\frac{2}{7}$
(h) $x = 5\frac{1}{3}, y = 5\frac{1}{3}$

2 (a) $x = {}^{-}1, y = 4$
(b) $x = 3, y = {}^{-}2$
(c) $x = 2, y = 0$
(d) $x = 3, y = {}^{-}1$

3 (a) $x = 3, y = {}^{-}1$
(b) $x = 8, y = 1$
(c) $x = 6, y = 4$
(d) $x = 3, y = 6$

4 (a) $x = 3.2, y = 1.4$
(b) $x = 1.4, y = {}^{-}2.4$

5 (a) $x = {}^{-}2, y = 5$
(b) $x = {}^{-}1.5, y = {}^{-}3.5$

6 (a) and (b) The graphs are parallel and so there is no solution.

The elimination method

Make sure that pupils carefully number each equation. Do make them state (1) + or – (2) on the left. Each solution should end with a 'sub in 1 (or 2)' or a 'check in 2 (or 1)'

If you start these simple elimination questions insisting on the correct method then the later equations will flow much more easily.

Exercise 13.4

1 $x = 2, y = 1$
2 $x = 3, y = 4$
3 $x = 5, y = 2$
4 $x = 1, y = 3$
5 $x = 3, y = 3$
6 $x = 3, y = 1$
7 $x = 3, y = 2$
8 $x = 4, y = 3$
9 $x = 1, y = 4$

Exercise 13.5

1 $x = 1, y = 2$
2 $x = 2, y = 1$
3 $x = 3, y = 2$
4 $x = 4, y = 3$
5 $x = 2, y = 5$
6 $x = 4, y = 1$
7 $x = 3, y = {}^{-}1$
8 $x = {}^{-}2, y = 5$
9 $x = {}^{-}1, y = {}^{-}3$

The re-arrangement and substitution methods

There is more than one correct way of solving these problems. The exercise should be accompanied by discussion about which method is the most suitable one to use.

Exercise 13.6

1 $x = 1, y = 3$
2 $x = 2, y = 7$
3 $x = {}^{-}2, y = 3$
4 $x = {}^{-}1, y = {}^{-}3$
5 $x = 1.5, y = {}^{-}3$
6 $x = \frac{3}{5}, y = \frac{{}^{-}1}{5}$
7 $x = 1\frac{1}{4}, y = 11\frac{1}{2}$
8 $x = 7, y = {}^{-}2\frac{1}{2}$
9 $x = 1.5, y = 45$
10 $x = 2\frac{2}{7}, y = {}^{-}1\frac{5}{7}$
11 $x = 3\frac{3}{5}, y = 15$
12 $x = 3\frac{1}{2}, y = {}^{-}4$

Exercise 13.7

1 10 and 15
2 12 and 16
3 £60, £85
4 $10\frac{1}{2}, 6\frac{1}{2}$

The next few problems are solved by forming one equation for the total number of items and the other for the total price.

5 (a) $c = 6, g = 14$
(b) 6 Coxs and 14 Granny Smiths

6 (a) $p = 14, s = 28$
(b) 98p

7 (a) $c = 45, m = 60$
(b) £1.05

8 (a) $x = 12, y = 16$

(b) $192\,\text{cm}^2$

9 $m = 3, c = {}^-2$

10 670

Extension Exercise 13.8

1 $x = 5, y = {}^-1, z = 3$

2 $a = 4\frac{1}{2}, b = 2, c = \frac{1}{2}$

3 $a = 2, b = {}^-3, c = 0$

This is a taxing question! Every time pupils combine equations they will reach one of the other given equations. In this case, they will need to use trial and improvement. Trying $c = 0$ is a logical start.

4 13

5 (a) $3a + 6b + c = 159$

$a + 7b + 2c = 218$

$2a + 7b + c = 155$

$a = 12, b = 8, c = 75$

(b) 1 apple, 8 bananas and 1 coconut cost £1.51

6 7, 7 and 17

7 (a) (i) Two of them combine to make the third.

(ii) No

(b) (i) Combine two and you get a different value for one unknown.

(ii) No solution

8 $x = 1, y = 2, z = 0$

Summary Exercise 13.9

1 (a) $x = 0.7, y = 5.3$

(b) $x = 8.4, y = 9.2$

(c) $x = 6, y = 0$

(d) They are parallel.

2 (a) $x = 3, y = 1$

(b) $x = 5, y = {}^-1$

(c) $x = {}^-2, y = 3$

(d) $x = 2, y = {}^-1$

(e) $x = 1, y = {}^-1$

(f) $x = 5, y = 1$

3 Yellow dusters are 50p; white dishcloths are 40p.

4 7 plain sparklers and 3 coloured sparklers

Activity: Trigon dragon patrol

This is an interesting investigation because it generates a simple formula, but with some limits.

1

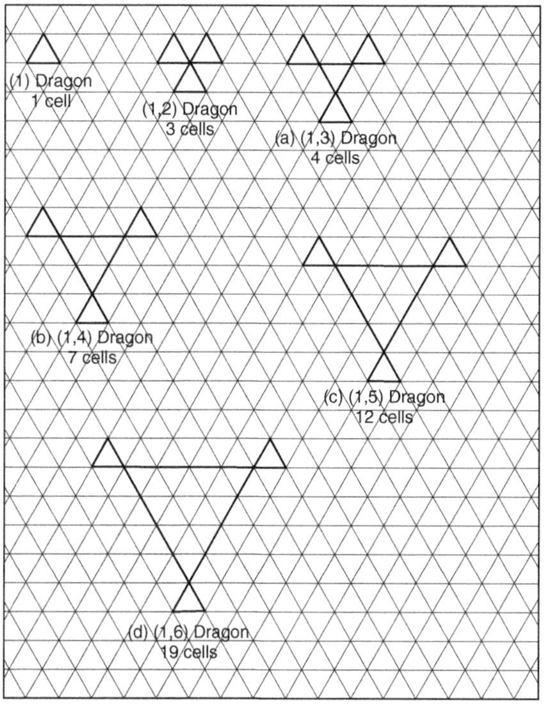

2 and 3 Learner dragon table:

Dragon	Units walked in one circuit	Dungeons guarded
(1, 1)	3	1
(1, 2)	9	3
(1, 3)	12	4
(1, 4)	15	7
(1, 5)	18	12
(1, 6)	21	19
(1, 7)	24	28

4

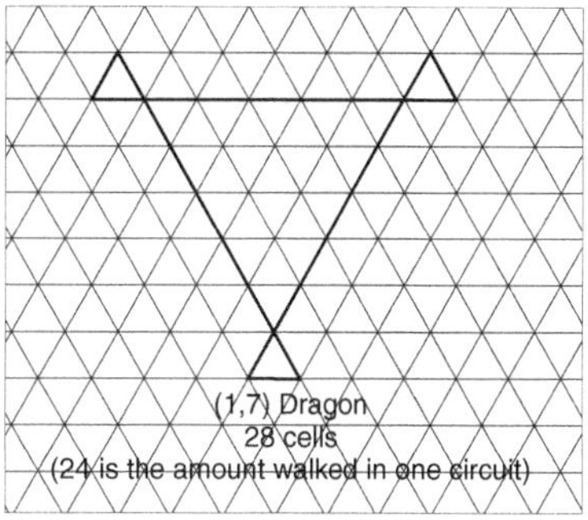

(1,7) Dragon
28 cells
(24 is the amount walked in one circuit)

5 A (1,10) dragon will guard 67 dungeons

6 $(n-2)^2 + 3$ when $n > 1$

7

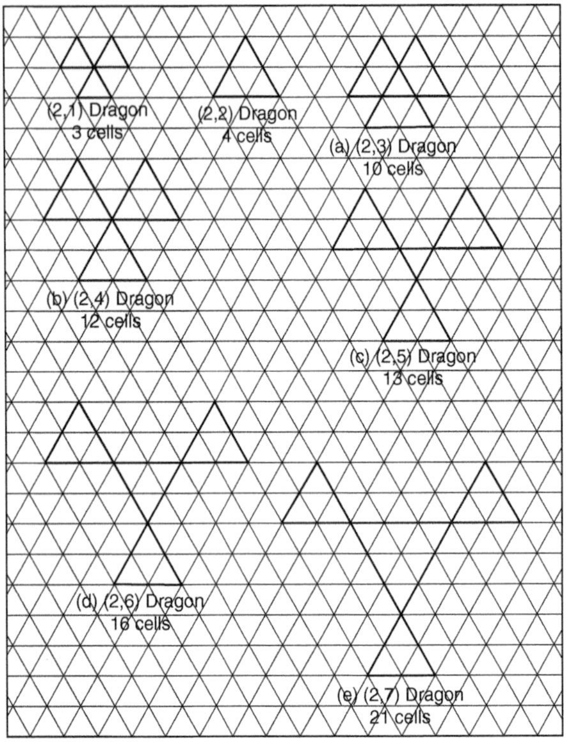

Dragon	Distance walked in one circuit (units)	Dungeons guarded
(2, 1)	9	3
(2, 2)	6	4
(2, 3)	15	10
(2, 4)	18	12
(2, 5)	21	13
(2, 6)	24	16
(2, 7)	27	21

8 A (2, 10) dragon will walk 36 units and guard 48 dungeons.
Formula for a megadragon:

$(n-4)^2 + 12$ when $n > 3$

9 $(n-2m)^2 + 3m$ when $n > 2m - 1$

14 Graphs

Exercise 14.1

1 (a) 50 km/h (b) 12.5 km/h (c) $8\frac{1}{3}$ km/h

Rose by car, George by bike and Camilla on foot (for example)

2 A vehicle travels for 30 minutes at 60 km/h and then stops for 15 minutes. It then goes for 30 minutes at 80 km/h and then stops for 45 minutes. The vehicle then returns, travelling for 45 minutes at 40 km/h, stops for 30 minutes then continues for 45 minutes at 53 km/h. The journey takes 4 hours.

3 (a) One is non-stop, one stops several times.

(b) 1 hour 18 minutes

(c) 50 km

(d) 70 km/h

(e) 50 km/h

4

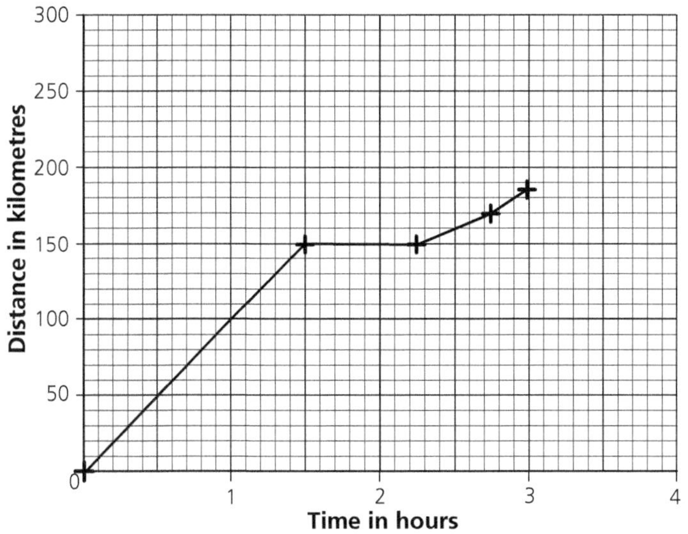

The journey was 185 km.

5

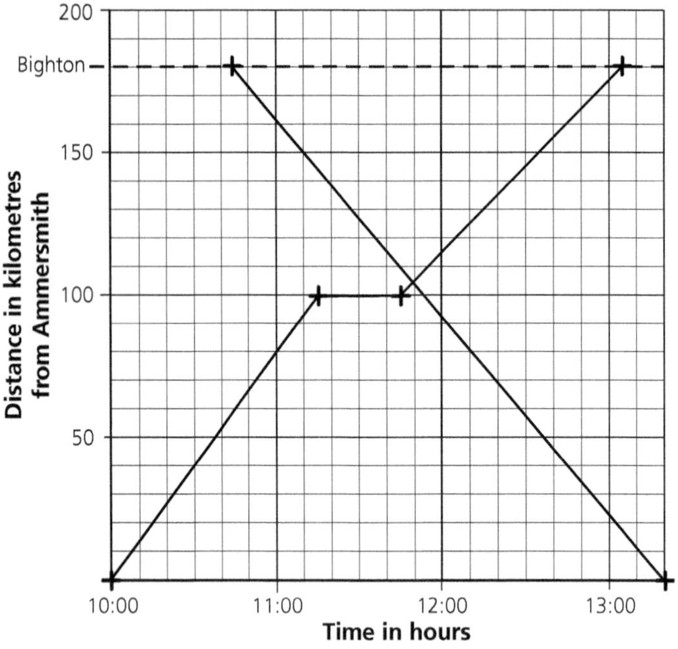

(a) 13:05

(b) She arrived at 13:20, the two cars passed at 11:50

6

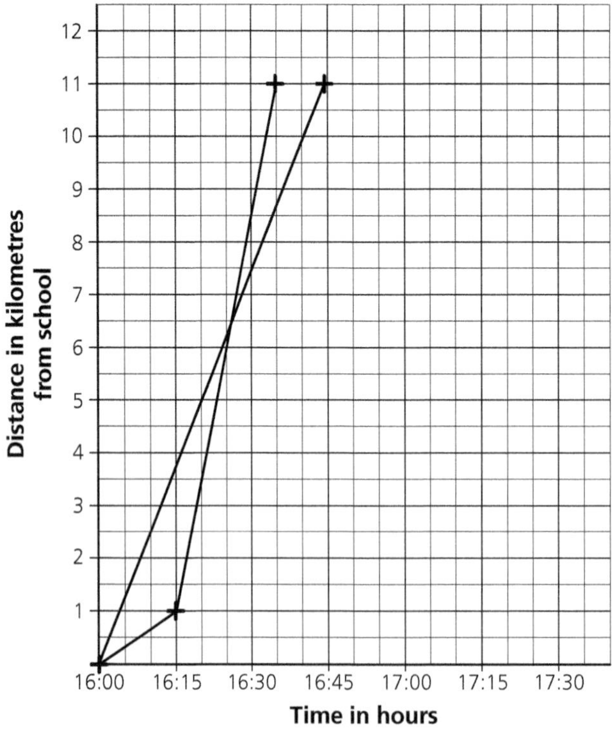

The bus overtakes the bicycle at 16:26

Exercise 14.2

1 (a) Check pupils' answers. Company A should be one whose sales patterns are affected by the summer season and to some degree around Easter. Company B could be one that is experiencing growth overall but experiences minor fluctuations from time to time.

(b) Answer depends on the pupils' answers to part **(a)**, the influence on April sales is likely to be the effect of Easter occurring around this time.

2 High sales from September, climbing until February, possibly dropping a little. Then climbing again in June, July and August as unwary tourists need to buy umbrellas.

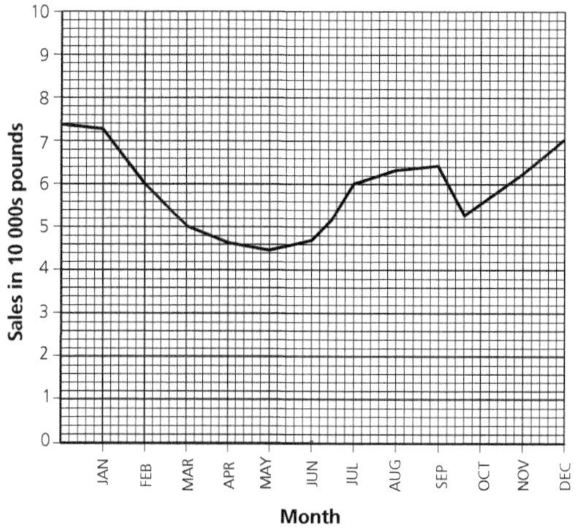

3 Company A sells computer software. Sales are fairly steady, with a few fluctuations. They rise again after August, as people come back from their holidays and start to pay attention to their IT requirements.

Company B sells ski clothes. There is very little sales activity over the summer months but as the skiing season approaches sales begin to increase.

Company C sells bicycles. The sales trend reflects people buying bicycles for the warmer months of the year (spring and summer) and the peak before Christmas could reflect present buying.

Company D sells swimwear. Sales increase during the summer months and fall away as the colder weather approaches.

4 (a) B (b) D (c) C (d) A

5 (a) C (b) D (c) B (d) A

Exercise 14.3

1 (a) (i) $y = 2x$

x	$^-2$	0	5
y	$^-4$	0	10

(ii) $y = {}^-3x$

x	$^-3$	0	1
y	9	0	$^-3$

(iii) $y = \frac{x}{2}$

x	$^-4$	0	10
y	$^-2$	0	5

(iv) $y = 5x$

x	$^-1$	0	2
y	$^-5$	0	10

(v) $y = -\frac{x}{4}$

x	$^-4$	0	8
y	1	0	$^-2$

(b)–(c)

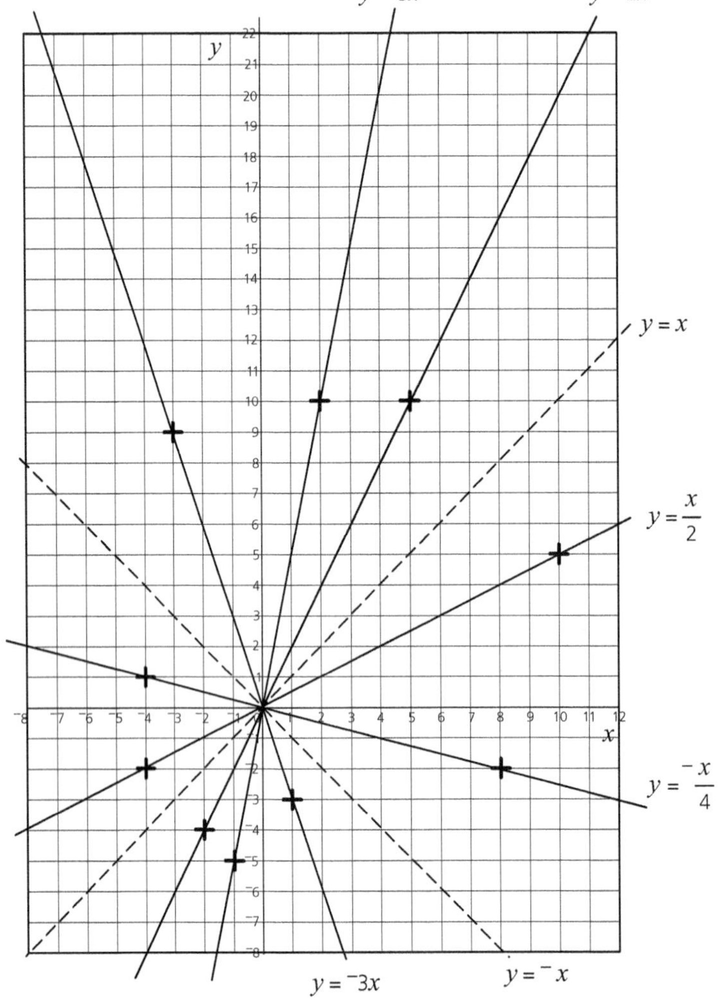

2 The graphs of $y = x$ and $y = {}^{-}x$ are at 45° to the axes (they are at 90° to each other). The negative graphs slope downwards and the positive graphs slope upwards to the right. Graphs of fractions of x are less steep. The higher the coefficient of x, the steeper the graph.

3 (a) (i) $y = 2x + 4$

x	⁻4	0	3
y	⁻4	4	10

(ii) $y = 3x - 2$

x	⁻1	0	3
y	⁻5	⁻2	7

(iii) $y = \frac{x}{2} + 3$

x	⁻4	0	10
y	1	3	8

(iv) $y = 5x + 2$

x	⁻1	0	1
y	⁻3	2	7

(v) $y = \frac{x}{4} - 3$

x	⁻4	0	8
y	⁻4	⁻3	⁻1

(b)

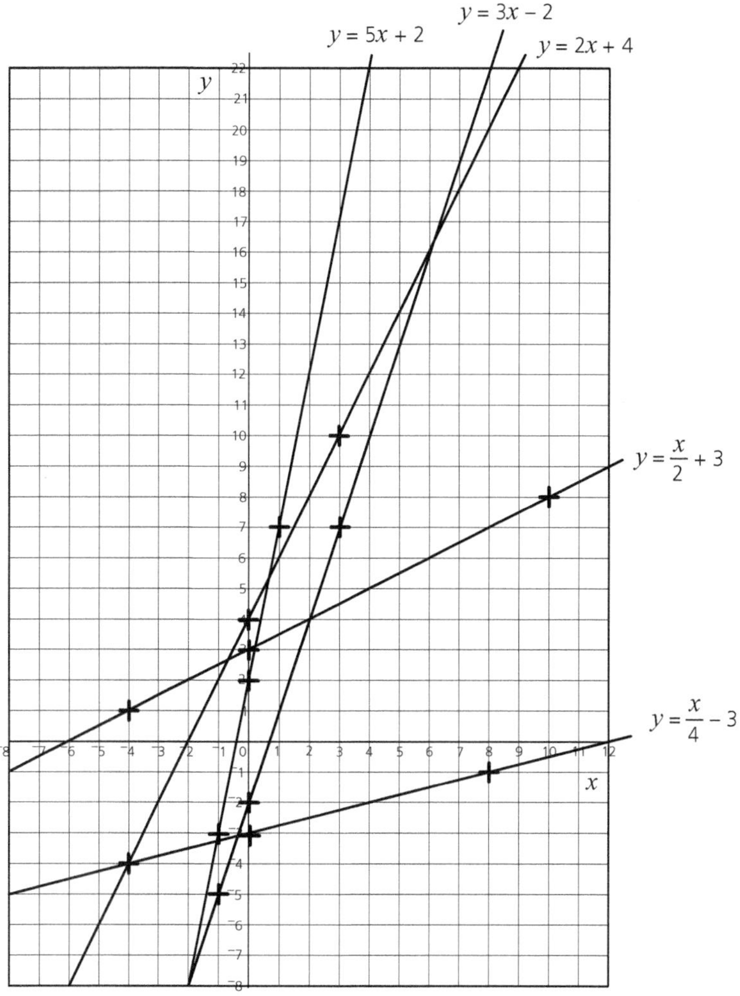

Graphs of curves

It is worth using a spreadsheet to demonstrate graphs of curves. By making the increments in x very small, say 0.25, you can clearly show how the gradient of the curve changes as it crosses the y-axis. This does need to be emphasised over and over again, to stop pupils using their rulers to draw graphs of curves!

Exercise 14.4

1 $y = x^2 - 1$

x	$^-3$	$^-2$	$^-1$	0	1	2	3
x^2	9	4	1	0	1	4	9
y	8	3	0	$^-1$	0	3	8

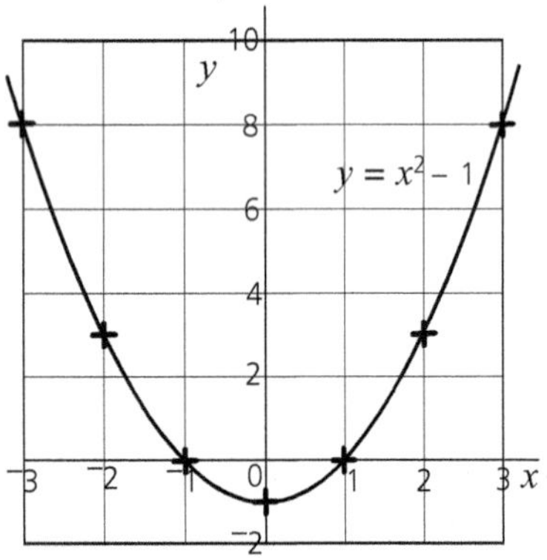

2 $y = x^2 + 2$

x	$^-3$	$^-2$	$^-1$	0	1	2	3
x^2	9	4	1	0	1	4	9
y	11	6	3	2	3	6	11

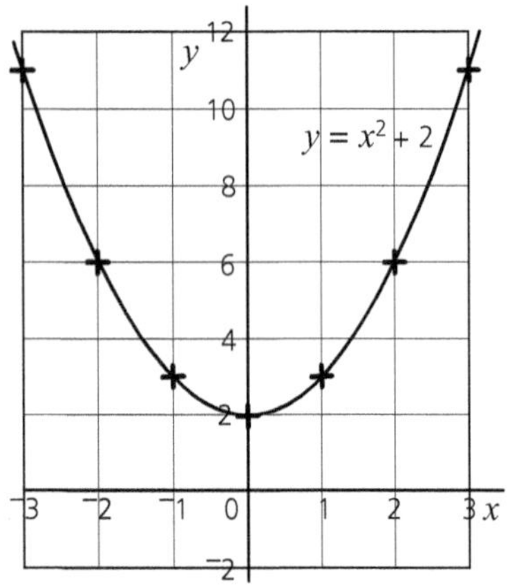

3 $y = 2x^2$

x	$^-3$	$^-2$	$^-1$	0	1	2	3
x^2	9	4	1	0	1	4	9
y	18	8	2	0	2	8	18

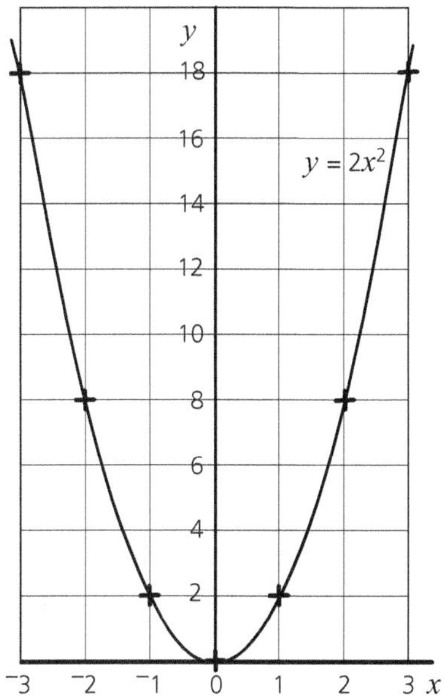

4 $y = \frac{x^2}{2}$

x	$^-3$	$^-2$	$^-1$	0	1	2	3
x^2	9	4	1	0	1	4	9
y	4.5	2	0.5	0	0.5	2	4.5

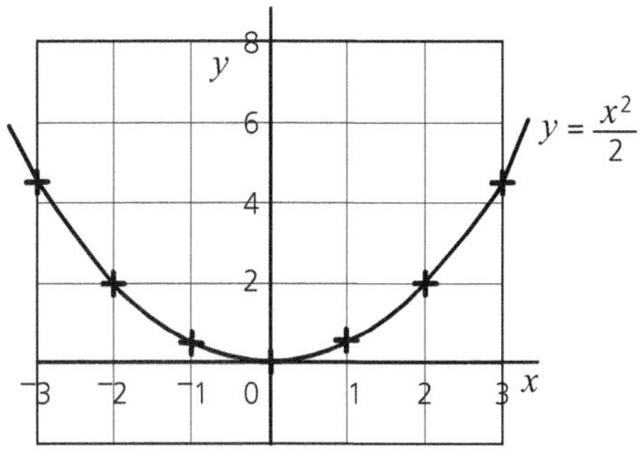

5 $y = 2x^2 - 3$

x	⁻3	⁻2	⁻1	0	1	2	3
x^2	9	4	1	0	1	4	9
y	15	5	⁻1	⁻3	⁻1	5	15

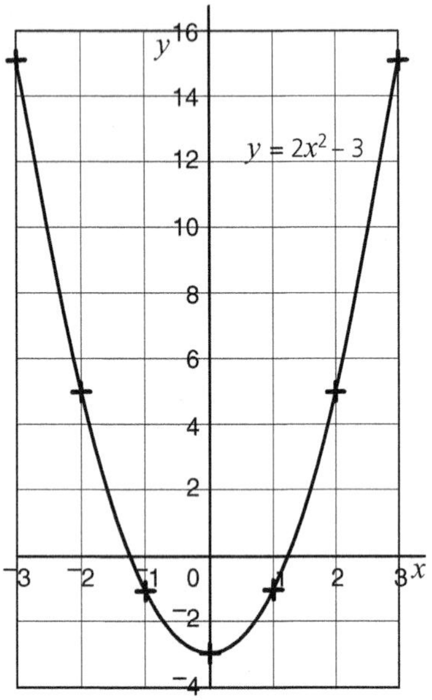

Exercise 14.5

1

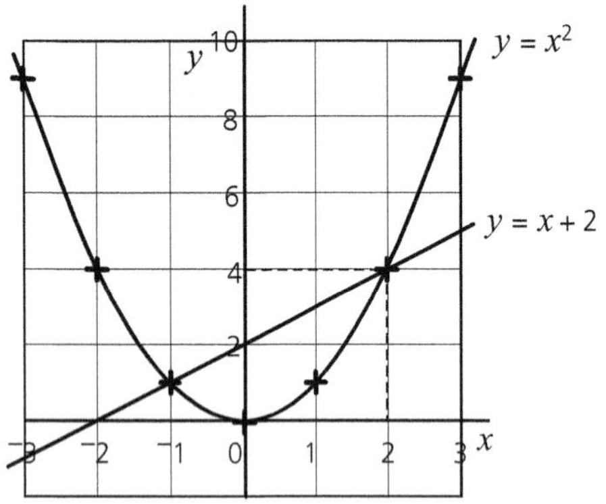

Lines intersect at (2, 4), (⁻1, 1)

2

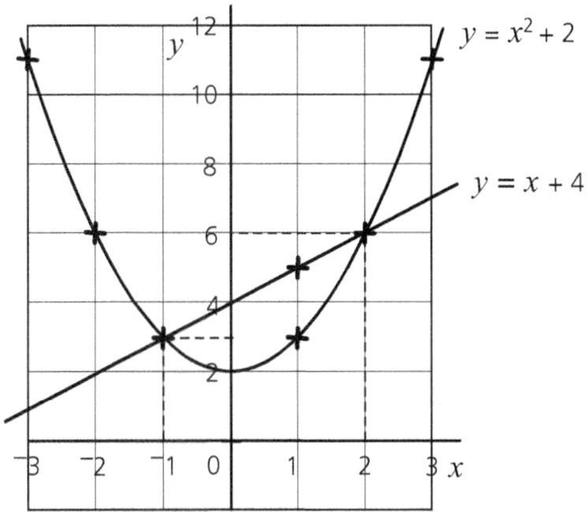

Lines intersect at (2, 6), (⁻1, 3)

3

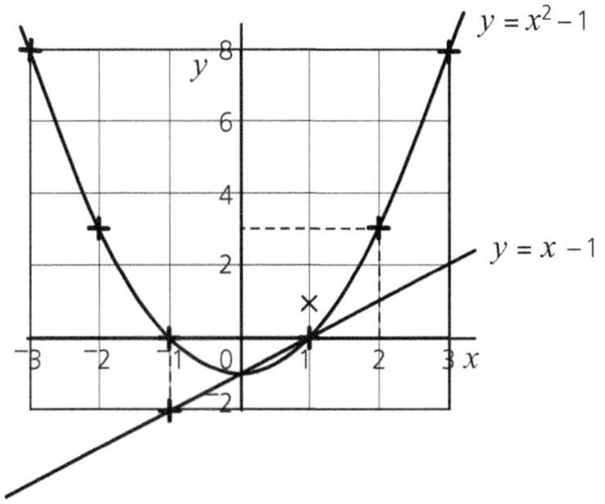

Lines intersect at (0, ⁻1), (1, 0)

4

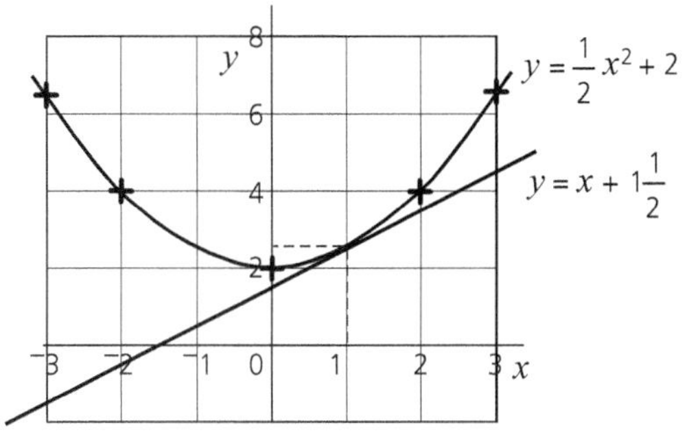

Lines intersect at $(1, 2\frac{1}{2})$ this line just touches the curve so only one result – a tangent!

5

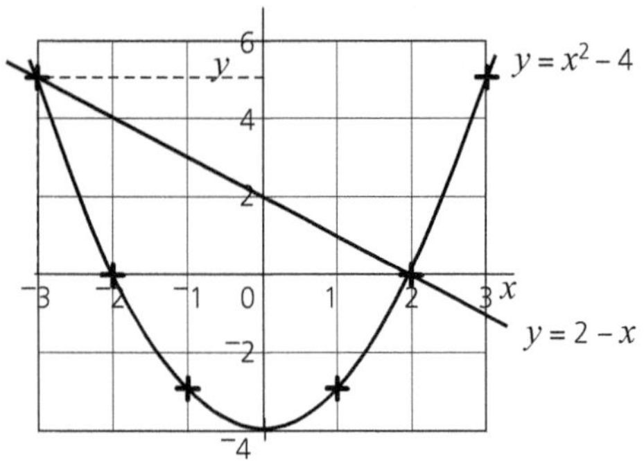

Lines intersect at ($^-3$, 5), (2, 0)

6

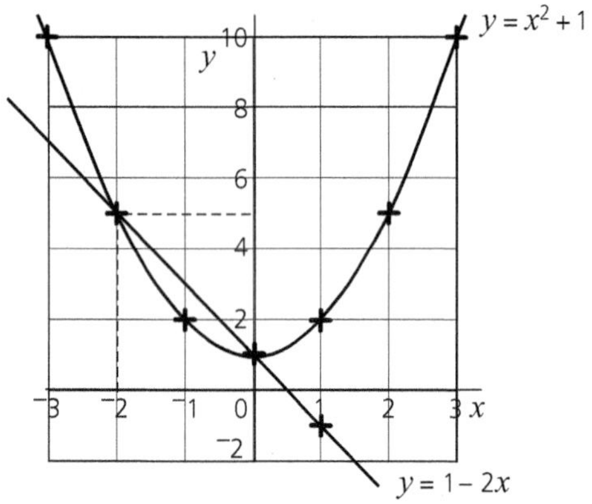

Lines intersect at (0, 1), ($^-2$, 5)

Extension Exercise 14.6

Although this is not a requirement of the syllabus, it is an interesting type of graph and one which pupils should be familiar with from their work in science.

1

x	$^-5$	$^-3$	$^-1$	$^-0.5$	$^-0.25$	0	0.25	0.5	1	3	5
y	$^-0.2$	$^-0.33$	$^-1$	$^-2$	$^-4$		4	2	1	0.33	0.2

$y = \frac{1}{x}$

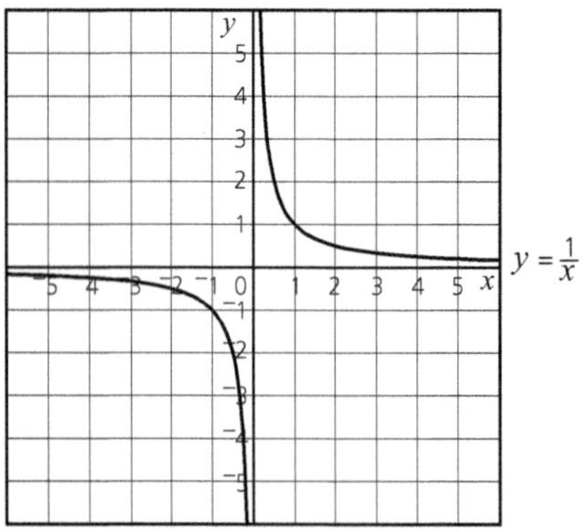

2 (a)

x	⁻4	⁻2	⁻1	0	1	2	4	6
y	⁻1	⁻2	⁻4		4	2	1	$\frac{2}{3}$

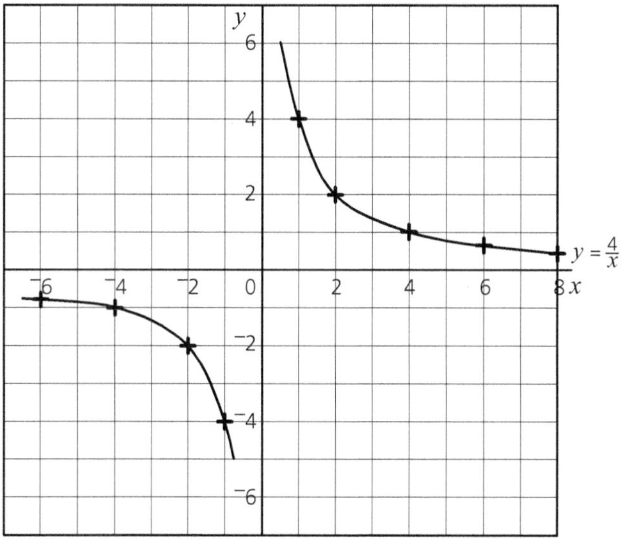

(b)

x	⁻6	⁻4	⁻2	0	2	4	6	8	10
y	⁻0.1	⁻0.125	⁻0.67	⁻0.25	⁻0.5		0.5	0.25	0.67

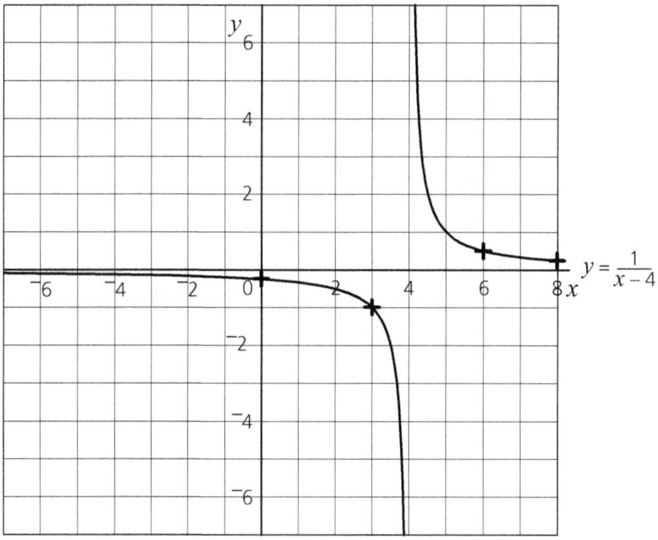

(c)

x	$^-3$	$^-2$	$^-1$	0	1	2	3	4
y	$\frac{1}{9}$	$\frac{1}{4}$	1		1	$\frac{1}{4}$	$\frac{1}{9}$	$\frac{1}{16}$

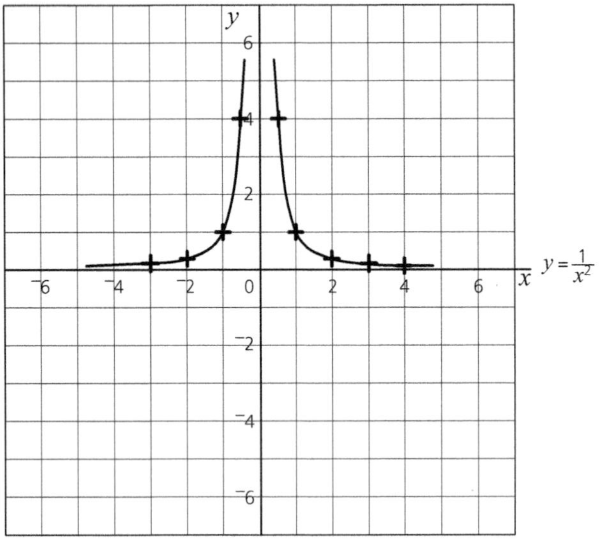

(d)

x	$^-5$	$^-1$	$^-0.5$	$^-0.25$	0	0.25	0.5	1	5
y	$^-0.1$	$^-0.5$	$^-1$	$^-2$		2	1	0.5	0.1

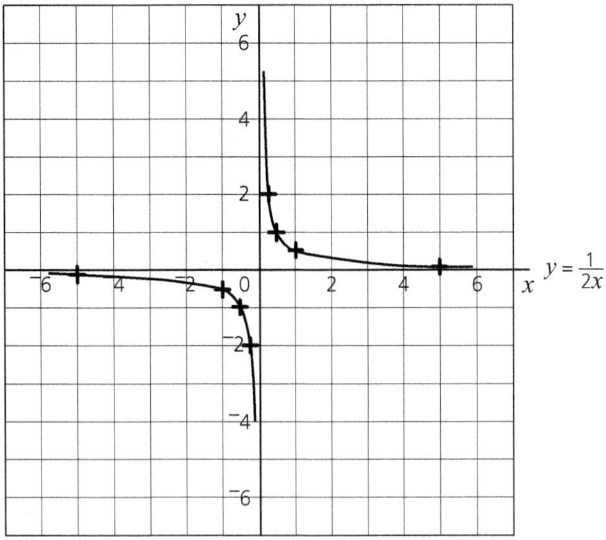

(e)

x	$^-2$	$^-1$	$^-\frac{1}{2}$	0	$\frac{1}{2}$	1	2	3	4	5
y	$\frac{1}{4}$	$\frac{1}{3}$	0.4	0.5	$0.\dot{6}$	1		$^-1$	$^-\frac{1}{2}$	$^-\frac{1}{3}$

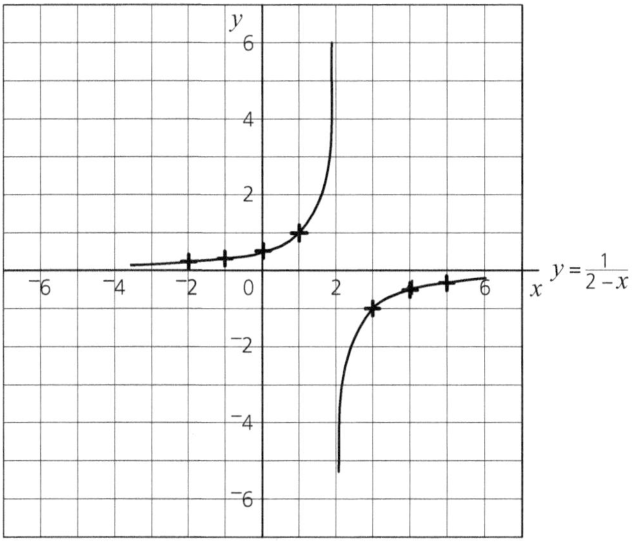

(f)

x	$^-3$	$^-2$	$^-1$	$^-\frac{1}{2}$	0	$\frac{1}{2}$	1	2	3	4
y	$^-\frac{1}{9}$	$^-\frac{1}{4}$	$^-1$	$^-4$		4	$^-1$	$^-\frac{1}{4}$	$^-\frac{1}{9}$	$^-\frac{1}{16}$

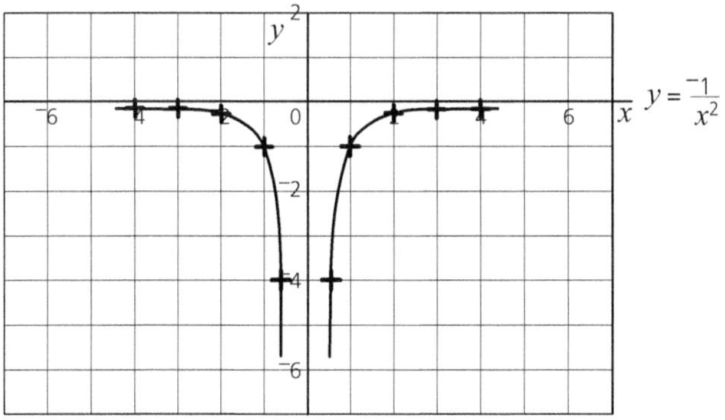

Extension Exercise 14.7

Again, these should be familiar from work in science.

1 $y = x^3$

x	$^-5$	$^-4$	$^-3$	$^-2$	$^-1$	0	1	2	3	4	5
y	$^-125$	$^-64$	$^-27$	$^-8$	$^-1$	0	1	8	27	64	125

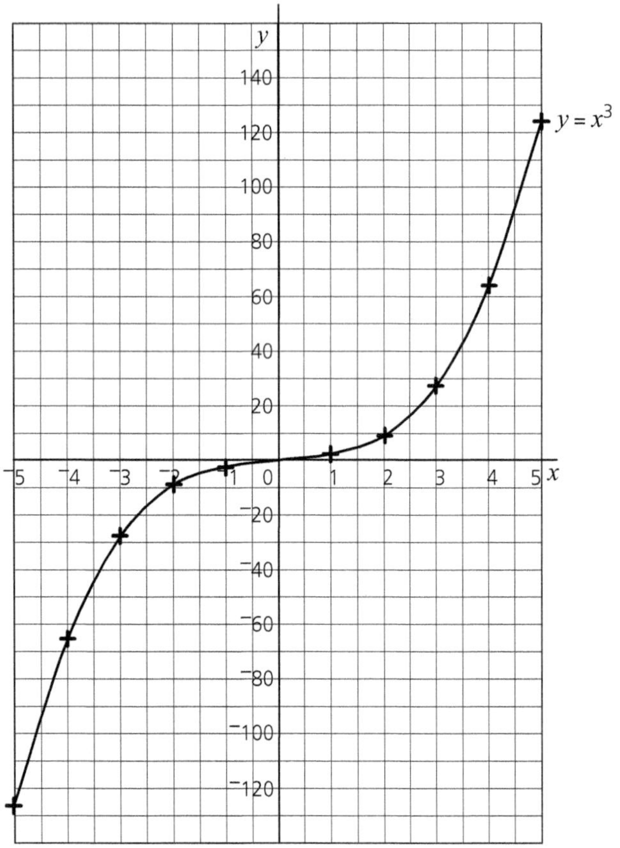

2 $y = x^2 - x$

x	$^-5$	$^-4$	$^-3$	$^-2$	$^-1$	0	1	2	3	4	5
x^2	25	16	9	4	1	0	1	4	9	16	25
y	30	20	12	6	2	0	0	2	6	12	20

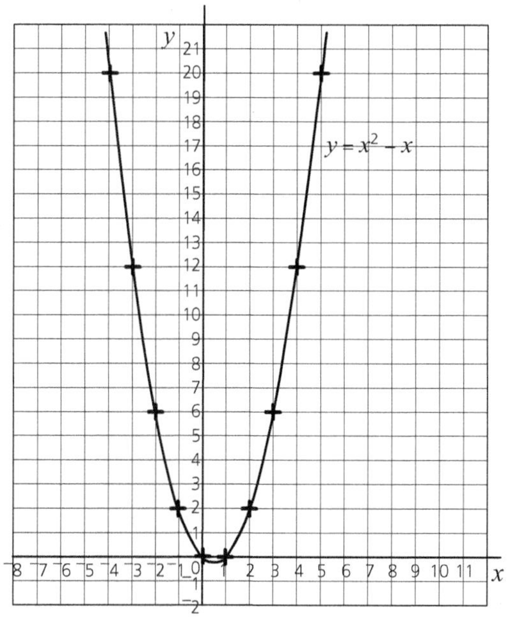

3 $y = x^2 + 2x$

x	$^-5$	$^-4$	$^-3$	$^-2$	$^-1$	0	1	2	3	4	5
x^2	25	16	9	4	1	0	1	4	9	16	25
y	15	8	3	0	$^-1$	0	3	8	15	24	35

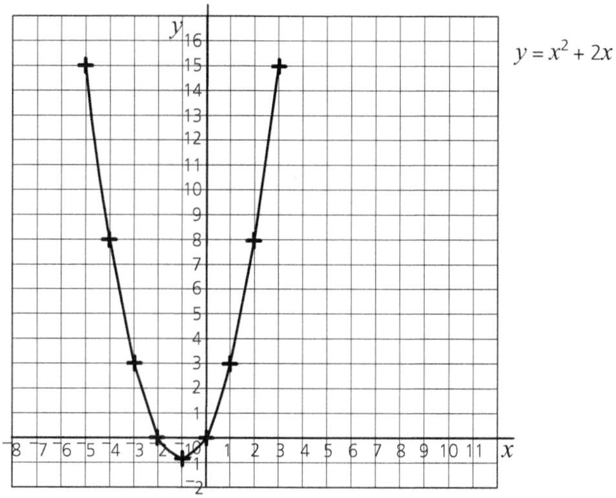

4 $y=\sqrt{x}$

x	⁻5	⁻4	⁻3	⁻2	⁻1	0	1	2	3	4	5
y	*	*	*	*	*	0	1	1.4	1.7	2	2.2

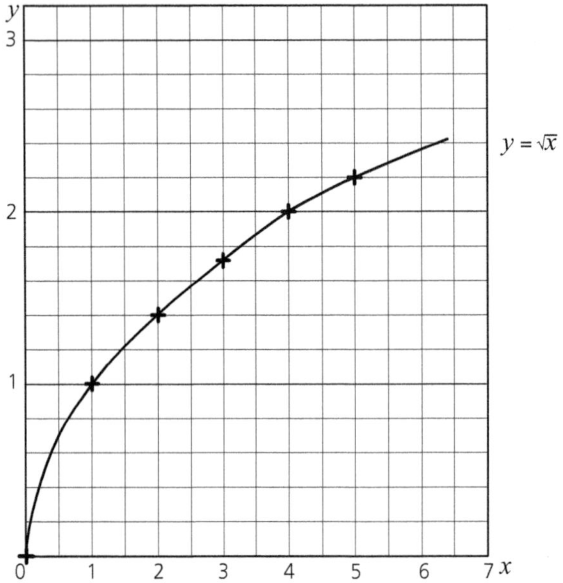

Summary Exercise 14.8

1 (a) 50 km/h

(b) Stopped for 1 hour

(c) 50 km/h

(d) 160 km/h

(e) Check pupils' answers, for example, shopping.

2 (a) $y = 2x - 4$

x	⁻2	⁻1	0	1	2
$2x$	⁻4	⁻2	0	2	4
y	⁻8	⁻6	⁻4	⁻2	0

(b)

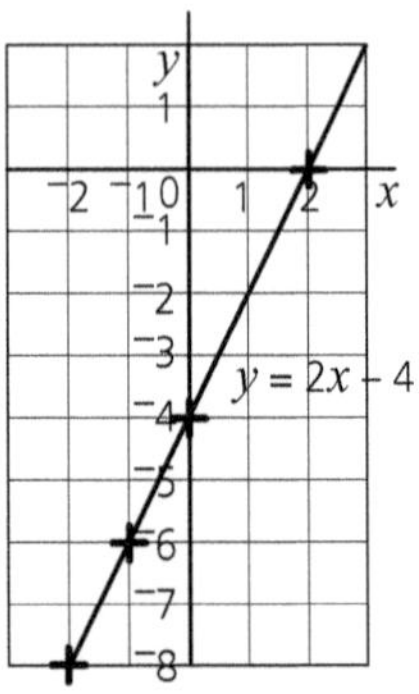

(c) (i) (2, 0)

(ii) (0, ⁻4)

(iii) (⁻1, ⁻6)

(iv) (⁻1, ⁻6)

3 (a) $y = x^2 - 1$

x	$^{-}3$	$^{-}2$	$^{-}1$	0	1	2	3
y	8	3	0	$^{-}1$	0	3	8

$y = x + 1$

x	$^{-}2$	$^{-}1$	0	1
y	$^{-}1$	0	1	2

(b)–(c)

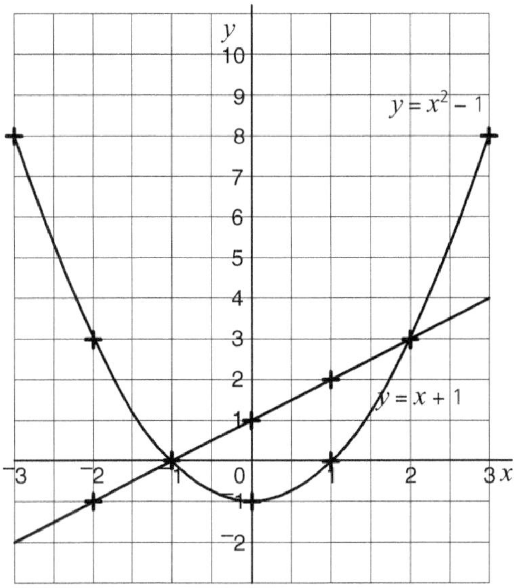

(d) Intersection at (2, 3), ($^{-}1$, 0)

Activity: Experiments and graphs

This Activity provides an opportunity for cross-curricular work with science. Try to encourage pupils to predict what their graph will look like. Some, like the distance travelled by the tip of a second hand of a clock, will look simple. But how will this graph compare to the distance traveled by second hands with different lengths? Plot them on the same graph. Pupils could plot the results of some of their scientific experiments. They will hopefully come up with their own ideas.

15 Equations and brackets

Most of this chapter deals with multiplying out two brackets. This is on the syllabus for some schools own scholarship papers, but not currently for ISEB Common Entrance or CASE.

Exercise 15.1

1 $9x + 3$

2 $8x - 20$

3 $10 - 6x$

4 $21 + 7x$

5 $12x + 30$

6 $3x^2 + x$

7 $8x^2 - 6x$

8 $5a^2 - 2ab$

9 $5ab + ac$

10 $12x - 9x^2$

11 $8x$

12 $10 - x$

13 $16x - 2$

14 $21 - 7x$

15 $15x - 7$

16 $3x^2 + 11x + 6$

17 $3a^2 - 3ab + 4a - 4b$

18 $a^2 - b^2$

19 $3 - 3x - 6x^2$

20 $2x^2 - 5xy + 2y^2$

Exercise 15.2

1 $x^2 + 5x + 4$

2 $x^2 + 5x + 6$

3 $x^2 + 10x + 24$

4 $x^2 + 14x + 49$

5 $x^2 + 2x + 1$

6 $x^2 + 7x + 12$

7 $x^2 + 6x + 8$

8 $x^2 + 6x + 9$

9 $x^2 + 11x + 24$

10 $x^2 + 9x + 14$

11 $x^2 - x - 2$

12 $x^2 + x - 6$

13 $x^2 - 4x - 5$

14 $x^2 - 16$

15 $x^2 + 2x - 3$

16 $x^2 + 4x - 12$

17 $x^2 + 11x + 28$

18 $x^2 - 9$

19 $x^2 + x - 20$

20 $x^2 - 1$

21 $x^2 - 3x + 2$

22 $x^2 - 6x + 8$

23 $x^2 - 8x + 15$

24 $x^2 - 8x + 7$

25 $x^2 - 4x + 4$

26 $x^2 + 2x - 8$

27 $^{-}x^2 + 5x - 6$

28 $x^2 + 5x + 6$

29 $x^2 - 6x + 9$

30 $x^2 - 4$

Exercise 15.3

1 $x^2 + 4x + 4$
2 $x^2 + 10x + 25$
3 $x^2 - 12x + 36$
4 $9 + 6x + x^2$
5 $16 - 8x + x^2$
6 $1 + 2x + x^2$
7 $x^2 + 8x + 16$
8 $x^2 - 4x + 4$
9 $x^2 + 20x + 100$
10 $x^2 - 16x + 64$

Exercise 15.4

1 $(x - 2)^2$
2 $(x + 3)^2$
3 $(x + 4)^2$
4 $(x - 1)^2$
5 $(x + 7)^2$
6 $(5 - x)^2$
7 $(10 + x)^2$
8 $(b - x)^2$
9 $(b - c)^2$
10 $(x + y)^2$
11 $(2x - 1)^2$
12 $(4x + 1)^2$
13 $(3x + 1)^2$
14 $(2x - 2)^2$
15 $(7x + 7)^2$
16 $(10 - x)^2$
17 $(10 + 2x)^2$
18 $(2b - x)^2$
19 $(3b - c)^2$
20 $(2x + 2y)^2$

Exercise 15.5

1 $x^2 - 100$
2 $x^2 - 81$
3 $121 - x^2$
4 $4x^2 - 25$
5 $9x^2 - 9$
6 $4a^2 - x^2$
7 $36 - a^2x^2$
8 $64 - \frac{x^2}{4}$
9 $a^2 - \frac{x^2}{4}$
10 $y^2 - \frac{x^2}{16}$

Exercise 15.6

1 $(x - 3)(x + 3)$
2 $(x - b)(x + b)$
3 $(x - 9)(x + 9)$
4 $(x - 4)(x + 4)$
5 $(x - 10)(x + 10)$
6 $(x - y)(x + y)$
7 $(2x - 1)(2x + 1)$
8 $(3x - 1)(3x + 1)$
9 $(4x - 1)(4x + 1)$
10 $(x - 2a)(x + 2a)$
11 $x^2 + 1$
12 $(2x - b)(2x + b)$
13 $(3x - 5)(3x + 5)$
14 $(12 - x)(12 + x)$
15 $81 + x^2$
16 $(5x - y)(5x + y)$
17 $(x - 3y)(x + 3y)$
18 $(x + 7y)(x - 7y)$
19 $(x + 4y)(x - 4y)$
20 $(6x - 11a)(6x + 11a)$

Exercise 15.7

1 $x = 0$ or 4

2 $x = 0$ or 4

3 $x = 0$ or $1\frac{1}{4}$

4 $x = {}^-4$ or 4

5 $x = 2$

6 $x = 5$

7 $x = 0$ or 4

8 $x = {}^-5$ or 5

9 $x = 0$ or $1\frac{2}{3}$

10 $x = {}^-10$ or 10

11 $x = {}^-4$

12 $x = 0$ or 3

13 $x = 0$ or ${}^-2\frac{1}{4}$

14 $x = {}^-6$ or 6

15 $x = 0$ or $\frac{3}{5}$

16 $x = {}^-7$

17 $x = 0$ or $\frac{5}{8}$

18 $x = {}^-2$ or 2

19 $x = 9$

20 $x = 0$ or $\frac{^-5}{7}$

21 $x = 4$

22 $x = 0$ or $1\frac{2}{3}$

23 $x = {}^-11$ or 11

24 $x = 3$

25 $x = 0$ or 9

26 $x = \frac{1}{2}$ or $\frac{^-1}{2}$

27 $x = {}^-8$

28 $x = 0$ or 15

29 $x = 4$

30 $x = {}^-3$

Extension Exercise 15.8

1 6 cm, 12 cm

2 5 cm, 20 cm

3 7, 13

4 9, 11

5 6, 9

6 5 cm, 5 cm

7 3 cm, 6 cm

8 (a) (i) $2n + 1$ (ii) always odd

(b) (i) 1 (ii) always 1 (odd)

(c) (i) $n^2 + n$ (ii) always even

9 (a) (i) $3n$ (ii) 3, 1 and n

(b) (i) $n^3 - n$ (ii) always even

10 (a) $p^2 - q^2$

(b) $p = 5, q = 4$

(c) (i) $p = 5, q = 3$ (ii) $p = 13, q = 12$

(d) (i) $3^2 + 4^2 = 5^2$ (i) $5^2 + 12^2 = 13^2$

when $(p + q)(p - q) = 144, p = 13, q = 5$

Summary Exercise 15.9

1 (a) $6 - 6x^2$ (b) $7b + 4$ (c) $^-a - 4$ (d) $2x^2 + 9$

2 (a) $x^2 + 4x + 3$ (c) $10 + 3b - b^2$

(b) $x^2 + 3x - 28$ (d) $5a - 5b + ab - a^2$

3 (a) $x^2 + 10x + 25$ (c) $25 - 10a + a^2$

(b) $x^2 - 12x + 36$ (d) $4a^2 - 4ab + b^2$

4 (a) $(x - 3)^2$ (b) $(a + 5)^2$

5 (a) $x^2 - 25$ (b) $x^2 - 49$ (c) $36 - a^2$ (d) $4a^2 - b^2$

6 (a) $(x - 6)(x + 6)$ (b) $(a - 12)(a + 12)$

7 35

8 8 cm and 11 cm

Activity: The dragon curve

The joy of this fractal for the prep school pupil is fairly obvious. It is very simple to generate but not quite as simple as it looks, because it matters how you fold the paper.

It can be quite hard, when working in pairs, to see exactly how to put the fractal together. It can generate a lot of discussion on clockwise, anticlockwise, rotation and reflection. When it becomes impossible to do mechanically one has to revert to the theory.

The basic table generates a sequence that leads to an unusual formula.

Large fractals can make a great classroom display!

Iteration	Number of lines	Number of points
0	1	2
1	2	3
2	4	5
3	8	9
4	16	17
5	32	33
6	64	65
n	2^{n-1}	$2^{n-1} + 1$

Practical materials

This exercise can be done with folded paper but it is difficult to stick down. It could be done simply by copying the fold onto centimetre-squared paper and using a different colour for each iteration. For an eye catching display, you can use pipe cleaners!

16 Probability

Exercise 16.1

1 (a) $\frac{1}{2}$ (b) $\frac{1}{4}$ (c) $\frac{10}{13}$ (d) $\frac{1}{13}$ (e) $\frac{3}{4}$ (f) $\frac{1}{52}$

2 (a) $\frac{1}{6}$ (b) $\frac{1}{3}$ (c) $\frac{1}{2}$ (d) $\frac{5}{6}$

3 (a) $\frac{5}{26}$ (b) $\frac{21}{26}$ (c) $\frac{4}{13}$

4 (a) $\frac{4}{11}$ (b) $\frac{2}{11}$ (c) $\frac{1}{11}$ (d) 0

5 (a) $\frac{11}{18}$ (b) $\frac{11}{18}$

6 (a) $\frac{3}{7}$ (b) 9

7 (a) $\frac{5}{12}$ (b) $\frac{5}{12}$

8 (a) $\frac{2}{5}$ (b) $\frac{1}{5}$ (c) $\frac{1}{5}$ (d) 0 (e) $\frac{11}{20}$ (f) $\frac{7}{10}$

Exercise 16.2

1 36

2 48

3 13 or 14

4 (a) 6 (b) 401

5 (a) 10 (b) Probably not, hairbrushes usually land bristles up.

6 (a) 10 (b) 30 (c) 20

7 (a) $\frac{1}{50}$ (b) 50 (c) 981

8 $\frac{3}{25}$ No

Exercise 16.3

1 (a) $\frac{2}{13}$ (b) $\frac{7}{13}$ (c) $\frac{2}{13}$ (d) $\frac{7}{26}$ (e) $\frac{1}{13}$ (f) $\frac{8}{13}$

2 (a) $\frac{1}{30}$ (b) $\frac{1}{5}$ (c) $\frac{1}{3}$ (d) $\frac{1}{2}$ (e) $\frac{8}{15}$

3 (a) (i) $\frac{5}{17}$ (ii) $\frac{4}{17}$

(b) (i) $\frac{7}{17}$ (ii) $\frac{4}{17}$

(c) (i) $\frac{3}{17}$ (ii) $\frac{6}{17}$

4 (a) $\frac{5}{12}$ (b) $\frac{5}{11}$ (c) $\frac{1}{2}$ (d) 5

5 (a) $\frac{7}{47}$ (b) $\frac{40}{47}$

6 (a) $\frac{10}{47}$ (b) $\frac{13}{47}$

7 (a) $\frac{2}{9}$ (b) $\frac{11}{26}$ (c) $\frac{12}{23}$

8 (a) $\frac{1}{4}$ (b) $\frac{59}{239}$

(c) (i) $\frac{1}{8}$ (ii) $\frac{30}{239}$

9 (a) $\frac{15}{32}$ (b) $\frac{5}{31}$ (c) $\frac{11}{31}$

10 (a) $\frac{10}{37}$ (b) $\frac{1}{4}$

(c) Genie took diamonds. You cannot tell what Aladdin took, except it was not diamonds.

(d) They both took emeralds or Aladdin took gold, emerald or diamond and the genie took silver.

Exercise 16.4

1

		First die					
		1	2	3	4	5	6
Second die	1	(1, 1)	(2, 1)	(3, 1)	(4, 1)	(5, 1)	(6, 1)
	2	(1, 2)	(2, 2)	(3, 2)	(4, 2)	(5, 2)	(6, 2)
	3	(1, 3)	(2, 3)	(3, 3)	(4, 3)	(5, 3)	(6, 3)
	4	(1, 4)	(2, 4)	(3, 4)	(4, 4)	(5, 4)	(6, 4)
	5	(1, 5)	(2, 5)	(3, 5)	(4, 5)	(5, 5)	(6, 5)
	6	(1, 6)	(2, 6)	(3, 6)	(4, 6)	(5, 6)	(6, 6)

(a) $\frac{1}{12}$ (b) $\frac{7}{12}$ (c) $\frac{1}{6}$ (d) $\frac{1}{2}$

2 (a) $\frac{5}{12}$ (b) $\frac{3}{4}$

3

		First die					
Second die		1	2	3	4	5	6
	1	(1, 1)	(2, 1)	(3, 1)	(4, 1)	(5, 1)	(6, 1)
	1	(1, 1)	(2, 1)	(3, 1)	(4, 1)	(5, 1)	(6, 1)
	1	(1, 1)	(2, 1)	(3, 1)	(4, 1)	(5, 1)	(6, 1)
	2	(1, 2)	(2, 2)	(3, 2)	(4, 2)	(5, 2)	(6, 2)
	2	(1, 2)	(2, 2)	(3, 2)	(4, 2)	(5, 2)	(6, 2)
	3	(1, 3)	(2, 3)	(3, 3)	(4, 3)	(5, 3)	(6, 3)

(a) $\frac{1}{12}$ (c) $\frac{1}{6}$ (e) $\frac{5}{9}$

(b) $\frac{11}{18}$ (d) $\frac{1}{18}$ (f) $\frac{4}{9}$

4 (a)

		First die					
Second die		1	2	3	4	5	6
	1	(1, 1)	(2, 1)	(3, 1)	(4, 1)	(5, 1)	(6, 1)
	2	(1, 2)	(2, 2)	(3, 2)	(4, 2)	(5, 2)	(6, 2)
	3	(1, 3)	(2, 3)	(3, 3)	(4, 3)	(5, 3)	(6, 3)
	4	(1, 4)	(2, 4)	(3, 4)	(4, 4)	(5, 4)	(6, 4)
	5	(1, 5)	(2, 5)	(3, 5)	(4, 5)	(5, 5)	(6, 5)
	6	(1, 6)	(2, 6)	(3, 6)	(4, 6)	(5, 6)	(6, 6)
	7	(1, 7)	(2, 7)	(3, 7)	(4, 7)	(5, 7)	(6, 7)
	8	(1, 8)	(2, 8)	(3, 8)	(4, 8)	(5, 8)	(6, 8)

(b) (i) $\frac{1}{16}$ (iii) $\frac{1}{8}$ (v) $\frac{19}{48}$

(ii) $\frac{1}{16}$ (iv) $\frac{1}{4}$

(c) 7, 8 and 9 are equally likely, each has a probability of $\frac{1}{8}$

5

		First spinner			
Secondspinner		1	2	2	3
	1	(1, 1)	(2, 1)	(2, 1)	(3, 1)
	2	(1, 2)	(2, 2)	(2, 2)	(3, 2)
	2	(1, 2)	(2, 2)	(2, 2)	(3, 2)
	3	(1, 3)	(2, 3)	(2, 3)	(3, 3)
	4	(1, 4)	(2, 4)	(2, 4)	(3, 4)
	4	(1, 4)	(2, 4)	(2, 4)	(3, 4)

(b) (i) 7 and 2

(ii) 4 or 5

(iii) $\frac{1}{2}$

(iv) $\frac{1}{2}$

(v) $\frac{1}{4}$

(vi) $\frac{5}{24}$

6 (a)

		First pile			
Second pile		A ♠	A ♥	A ♦	A ♣
	K ♠	A ♠ K ♠	A ♥ K ♠	A ♦ K ♠	A ♣K ♠
	K ♥	A ♠ K ♥	A ♥K ♥	A ♦K ♥	A ♣K ♥
	K ♦	A ♠ K ♦	A ♥K ♦	A ♦ K ♦	A ♣K ♦
	K ♣	A ♠ K ♣	A ♥K ♣	A ♦K ♣	A ♣ K ♣

(b) (i) $\frac{1}{4}$ (ii) $\frac{1}{2}$ (iii) $\frac{1}{4}$ (iv) 0

Extension Exercise 16.5

1

	Girls	Boys	Total
Pets	7	9	16
No pets	5	1	6
Total	12	10	22

(a) $\frac{6}{11}$ (b) $\frac{8}{11}$ (c) $\frac{9}{22}$

2 (a)

	Girls	Boys	Total
Board	60	70	130
Day	90	20	110
Total	150	90	240

(b) $\frac{1}{12}$ (c) $\frac{9}{11}$

3

	Coq au vin	Omelette	Total
Caramel	35	14	49
Glace	8	29	37
Total	43	43	86

(a) 8 (b) $\frac{29}{86}$

4 (a) 24 (b) $\frac{7}{12}$

5 (a)

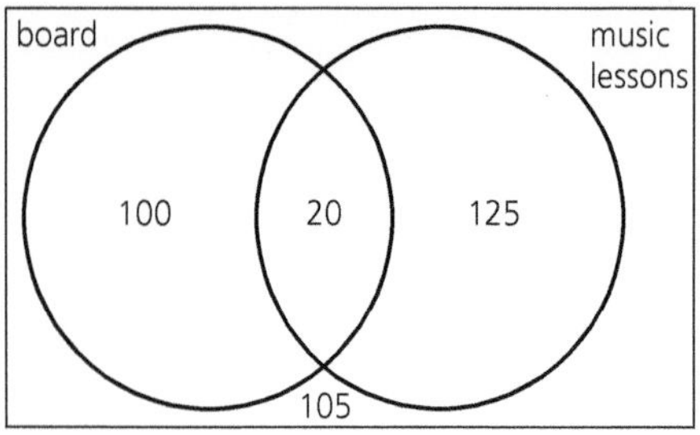

(b) $\frac{2}{7}$

6 (a)

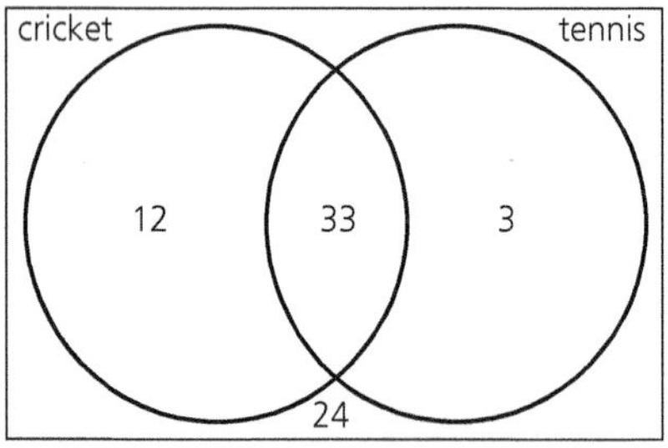

(b) $\frac{1}{6}$

7 (a) 26 (b) 1 (c) 5 (d) $\frac{15}{26}$

8 (a) 18 (b) $\frac{1}{18}$ (c) $\frac{1}{2}$

9 (a)

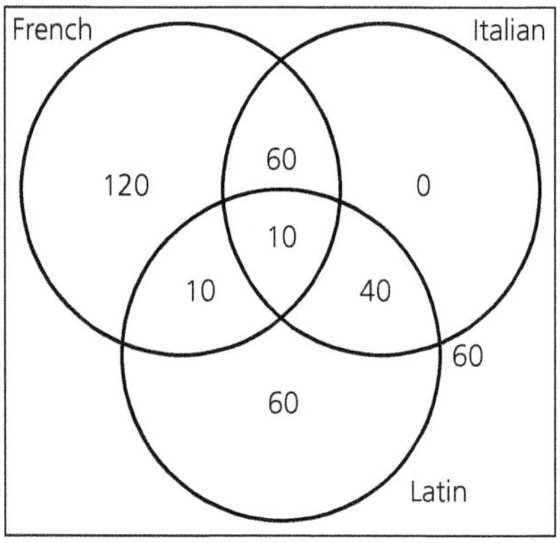

(b) $\frac{7}{36}$ (c) $\frac{1}{18}$

10 (a) $22 - x$

(b)

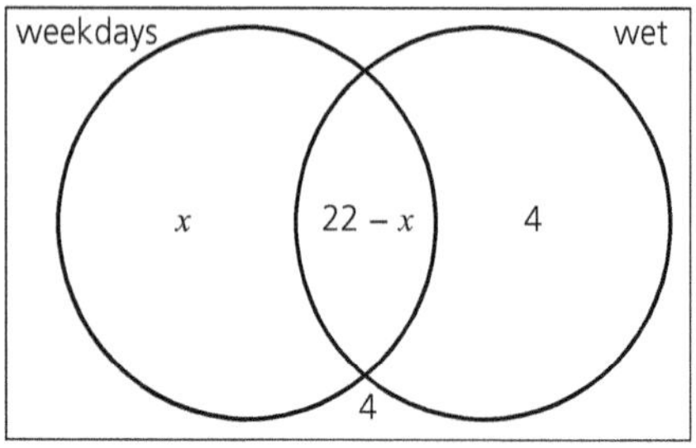

(c) (i) $\frac{22-x}{22}$ (ii) $\frac{x}{22}$

(d) $\frac{26-x}{30}$ (e) $\frac{26-x}{30} = \frac{1}{2}, x = 11$

11 (a) $95 - x$ (b) $135 - x$

(c)

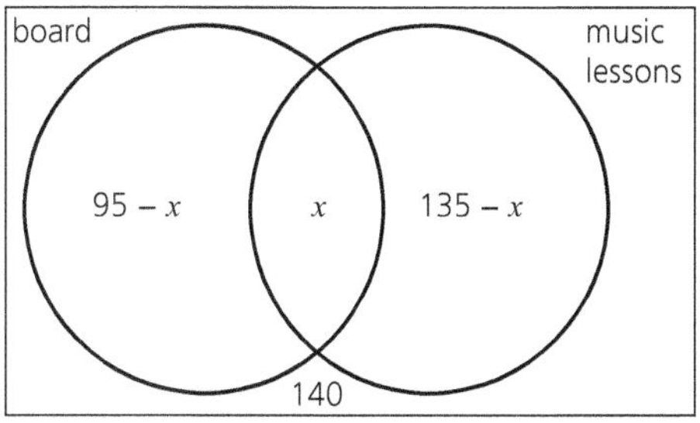

(d) 50

12 (a) $24 - x$

(b)

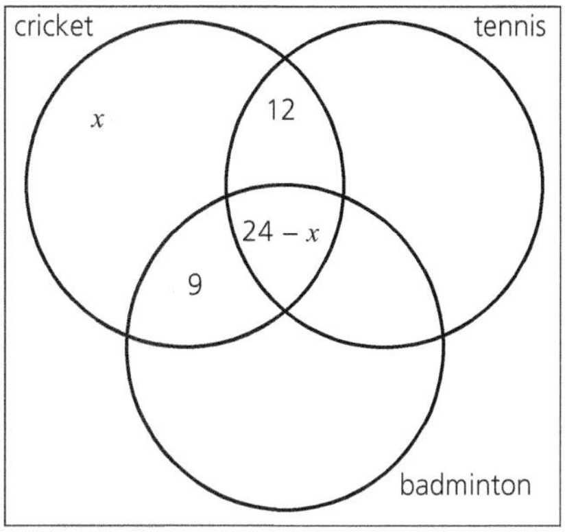

(c) $x + 17 = 36$ (As 36 boys play tennis, 36 do not play tennis) so $x = 19$

(d)

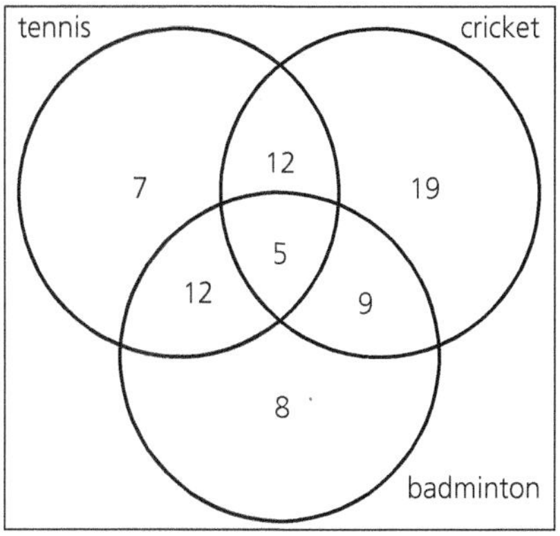

(e) $\frac{1}{6}$

Summary Exercise 16.6

1 (a) $\frac{1}{13}$ (c) $\frac{1}{52}$ (e) $\frac{4}{13}$

(b) $\frac{1}{4}$ (d) $\frac{2}{13}$

2 (a) $\frac{3}{8}$ (b) $\frac{1}{2}$ (c) $\frac{3}{4}$

3 (a)

		First die					
Second die		1	2	3	4	5	6
	1	(1, 1)	(2, 1)	(3, 1)	(4, 1)	(5, 1)	(6, 1)
	2	(1, 2)	(2, 2)	(3, 2)	(4, 2)	(5, 2)	(6, 2)
	3	(1, 3)	(2, 3)	(3, 3)	(4, 3)	(5, 3)	(6, 3)
	3	(1, 3)	(2, 3)	(3, 3)	(4, 3)	(5, 3)	(6, 3)
	5	(1, 5)	(2, 5)	(3, 5)	(4, 5)	(5, 5)	(6, 5)
	6	(1, 6)	(2, 6)	(3, 6)	(4, 6)	(5, 6)	(6, 6)

(b) (i) $\frac{1}{6}$ (ii) $\frac{11}{36}$ (iii) $\frac{25}{36}$ (iv) $\frac{1}{12}$

(c) 5

4 (a) $\frac{3}{10}$ (b) $\frac{2}{9}$ (c) $\frac{1}{3}$ (d) 8

5 9

6 (a)

	Prep set	No prep set	Total
Asked for	56	14	70
Not asked for	24	6	30
Total	80	20	100

(i) 6% (ii) 24% (iii) 14%

(b) 2 or more likely 3

7 (a) $75 - x$

(b)

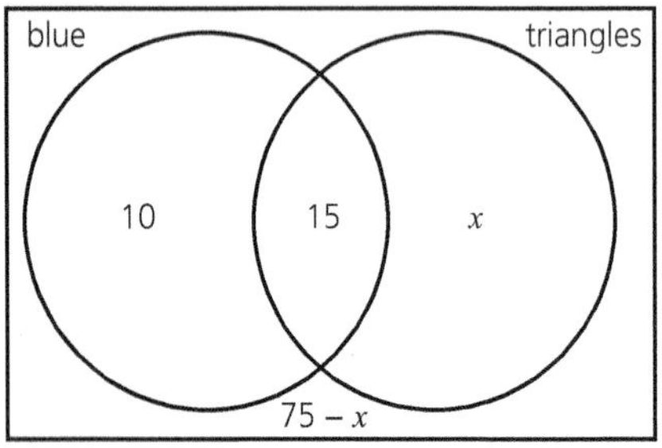

(c) The equation is: $\frac{75-x}{100} = \frac{15}{25}$, $x = 15$, total number of triangles = 30

Activity: Random cricket

Feel free to adjust the game if you have no cricketers.

17 Transformation geometry

This chapter takes a more formal approach to transformations, including the construction of reflections and rotations. The aim is to encourage pupils to see beyond the obvious.

Exercise 17.1

1 (a)

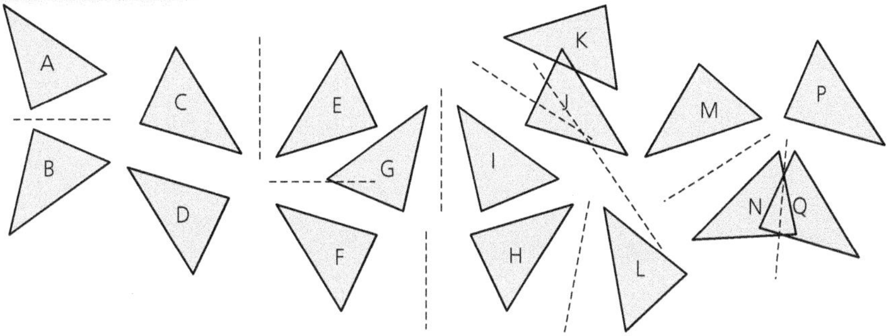

(b) A and B, C and E, E and F, G and I, I and K, M and N, H and M, N and Q, F and H, H and L

2

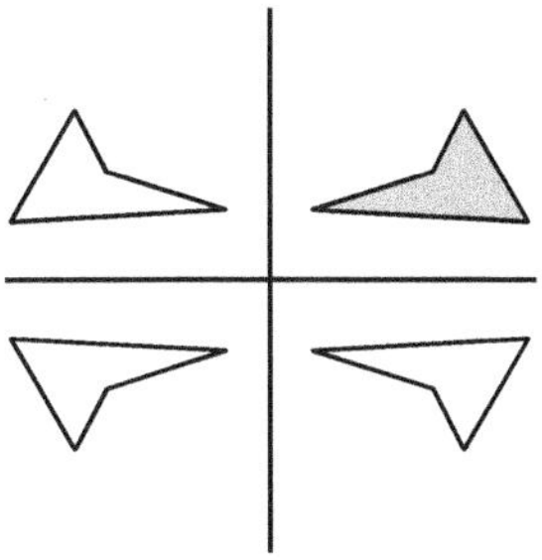

3

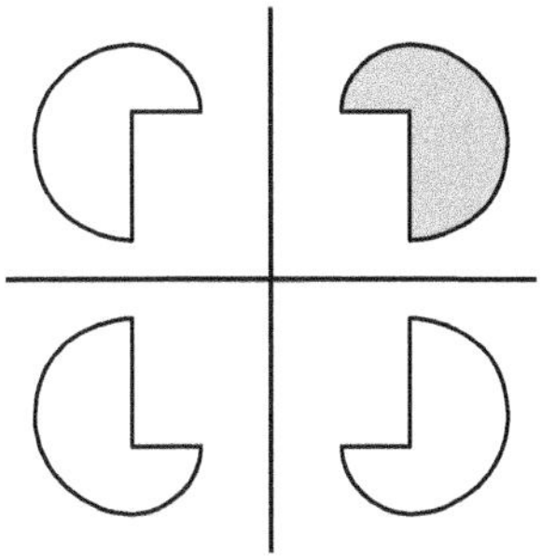

4 **(a)** **(b)** Check pupils' own drawings.

5 Check pupils' own designs.

Exercise 17.2

1 Check pupils' drawings, which should look similar to this.

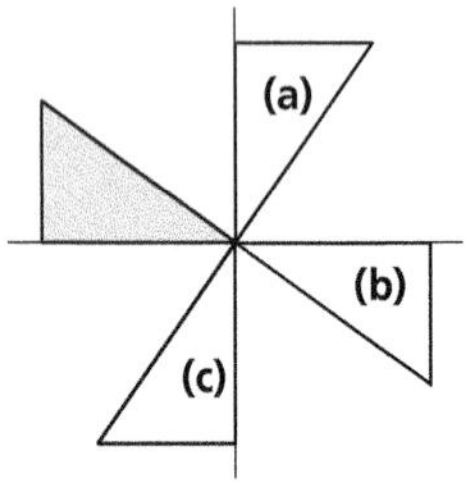

2 Check pupils' drawings, which should look similar to this.

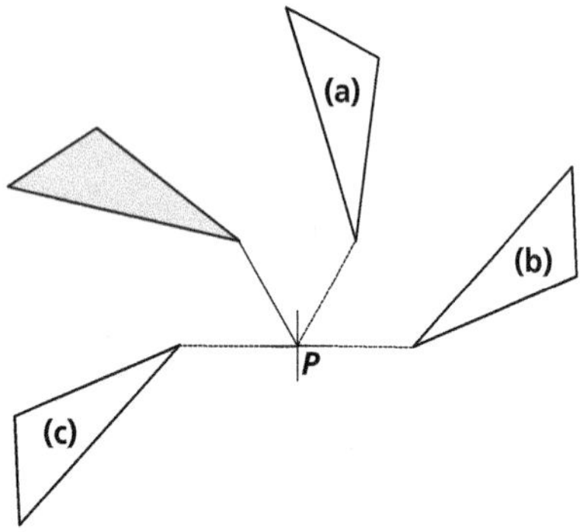

3 Check pupils' drawings, which should look similar to this.

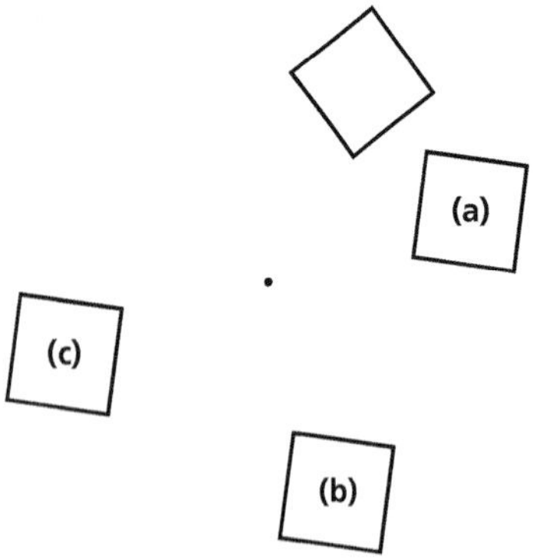

4 Check pupils' own drawings.

Exercise 17.3

1 **(a)** Order of rotational symmetry 2, lines of symmetry: 2

(b) Order of rotational symmetry 2, lines of symmetry: 2

(c) Order of rotational symmetry 4, lines of symmetry: 4

(d) Order of rotational symmetry 0 (none), lines of symmetry: 1

(e) Order of rotational symmetry 0 (none), lines of symmetry: 1

2 (a) Order of rotational symmetry 0 (none), lines of symmetry: 1

(b) Order of rotational symmetry 2, lines of symmetry: 2

(c) Order of rotational symmetry 6, lines of symmetry: 0

(d) Order of rotational symmetry 2, lines of symmetry: 2

(e) Order of rotational symmetry 3, lines of symmetry: 3

3 (a) Order of rotational symmetry 2, lines of symmetry: 0

(b) Order of rotational symmetry 2, lines of symmetry: 2

(c) Order of rotational symmetry 4, lines of symmetry: 0

(d) Order of rotational symmetry 0 (none), lines of symmetry: 0

(e) Order of rotational symmetry 3, lines of symmetry: 0

4 In questions 4–6 the answers given are examples – they are not the only possible answers.

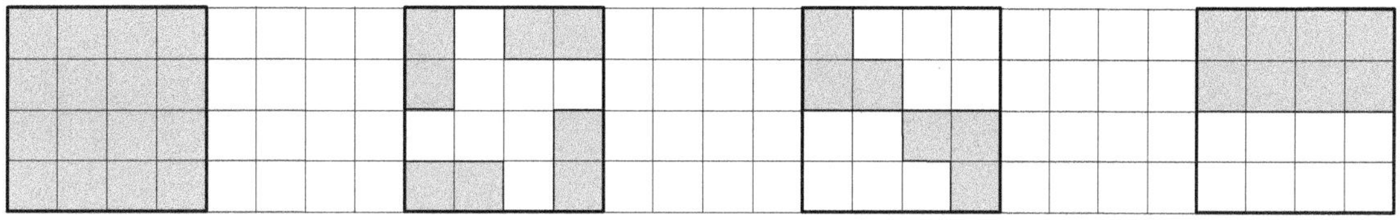

4 lines of symmetry, rotational symmetry of order 4

0 lines of symmetry, rotational symmetry of order 4

0 lines of symmetry, rotational symmetry of order 2

1 lines of symmetry and no rotational symmetry

5

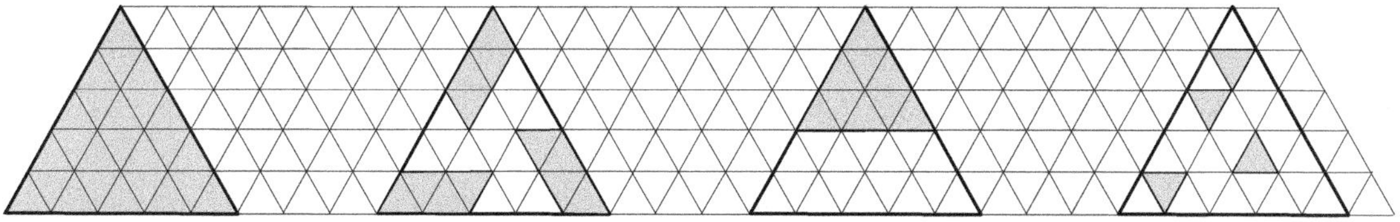

3 lines of symmetry, rotational symmetry of order 3

0 lines of symmetry, rotational symmetry of order 3

1 line of symmetry and no rotational symmetry

No lines of symmetry and no rotational symmetry

6

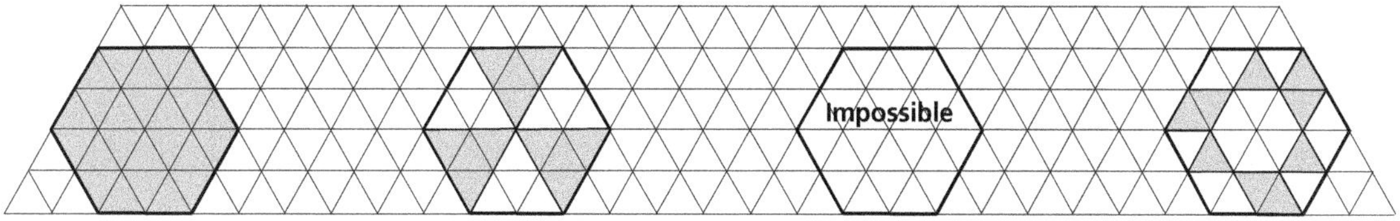

6 lines of symmetry, rotational symmetry of order 6

3 lines of symmetry, rotational symmetry of order 3

3 lines of symmetry and no rotational symmetry

0 lines of symmetry, rotational symmetry of order 3

7

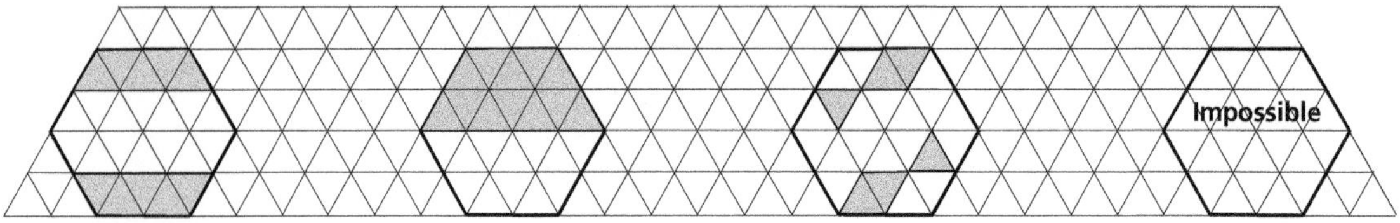

Exercise 17.4

1

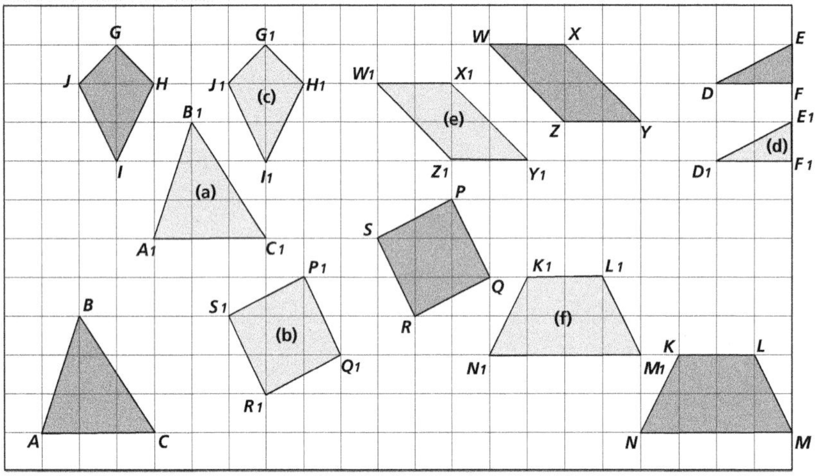

2 (a)

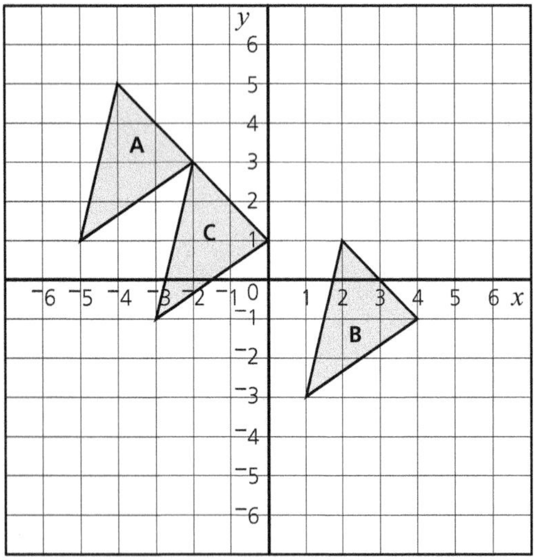

(b) (1, ⁻3), (2, 1) and (4, ⁻1)

(c) (⁻3, ⁻1), (⁻2, 3) and (0, 1)

(d) A translation of 2 left and 2 up

3 (a) $A'(1, 6)$

(b) $B'(^-2, 1)$

(c) $C'(^-1, -1)$

(d) $D'(^-3, 3)$

(e) $E'(2, ^-5)$

Exercise 17.5

1 Scale factor × $\frac{1}{2}$, centre of enlargement $(^-1, 1)$

2 Scale factor × 2, centre of enlargement (5, 3)

3 Scale factor × 3, centre of enlargement $(3, ^-4)$

4 Scale factor × $\frac{1}{2}$, centre of enlargement $(^-2, ^-2)$

5

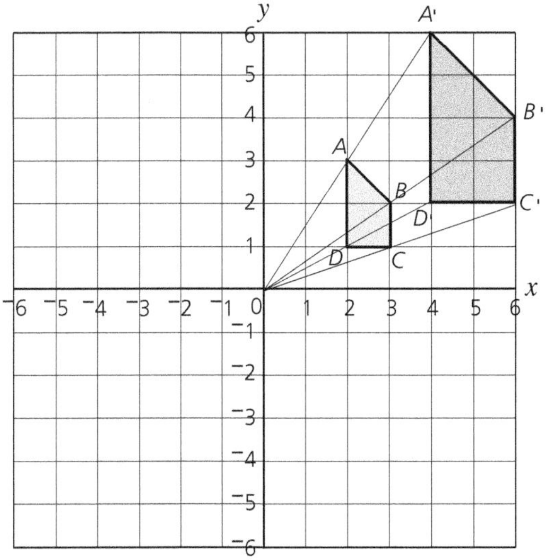

6

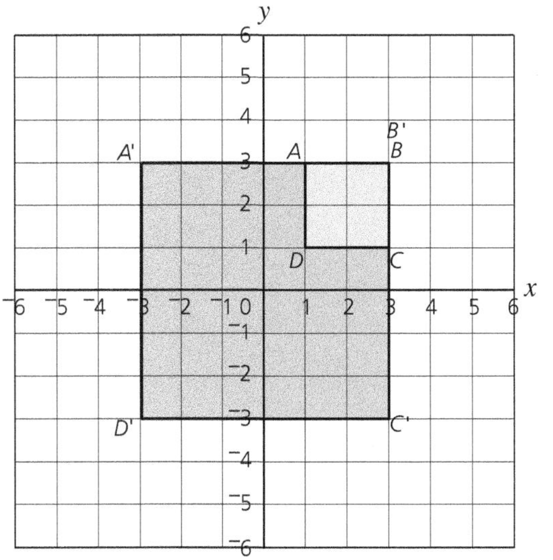

7

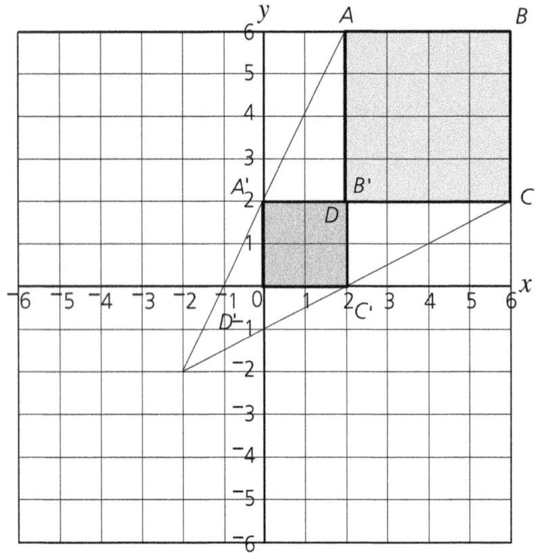

8

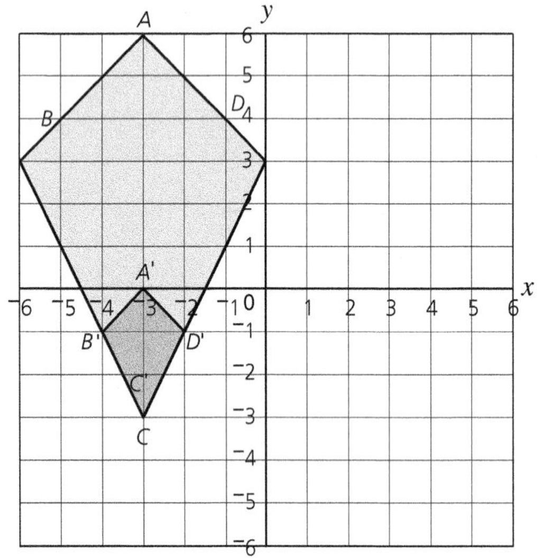

Exercise 17.6

1 **(a)** A reflection in the line $y = 1.5$

(b) A reflection in the line $x = {}^{-}1$

or a rotation of 180° about the point $({}^{-}1, {}^{-}2)$

or a rotation of 90° clockwise about the point $({}^{-}1, {}^{-}6)$

or a rotation of 90° anticlockwise about the point $({}^{-}1, 2)$

(c) A translation by 8 units right and 3 units down

(d) An enlargement of scale factor 2 and centre (0, 1)

(e) An enlargement of scale factor $\frac{1}{2}$ and centre (0, 1)

2 **(a)** A reflection in the line $y = 2$

or a rotation of 180° about the point $(^-4, 2)$

(b) A translation by 6 units left and 2 up

(c) A rotation of 90° clockwise about the point $(^-4, ^-2)$

or a reflection in $y = x + 2$

(d) An enlargement of scale factor 2 and centre $(^-5, ^-2)$

(e) a rotation of 90° clockwise about the point $(2, ^-2)$

or a reflection in the line $y = {}^-x$

3 **(a)** A translation by 6 units left and 2 down

(b) A rotation of 180° about the point $(^-3.5, 2)$

(c) An enlargement of scale factor 2 and centre $(^-5, 3)$

(d) An enlargement of scale factor $\frac{1}{2}$ and centre $(^-5, 3)$

(e) A reflection in the line $y = x$

(f) A rotation of 90° anticlockwise about the point $(^-1, 1)$

4 **(a)** A reflection in the line $x = 1$

(b) A rotation of 90° anticlockwise about the point $(1, ^-1)$

(c) An enlargement of scale factor $\frac{1}{2}$ and centre $(1, 1)$

(d) A translation by 1 unit left and 6 down

(e) A reflection in the line $y = {}^-x$

5 **(a)–(c)**

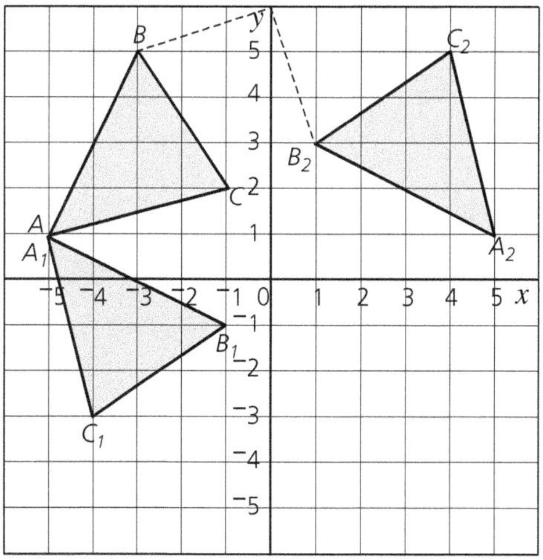

(d) A rotation of 90° anticlockwise about (0, 6)

6 (a)–(c)

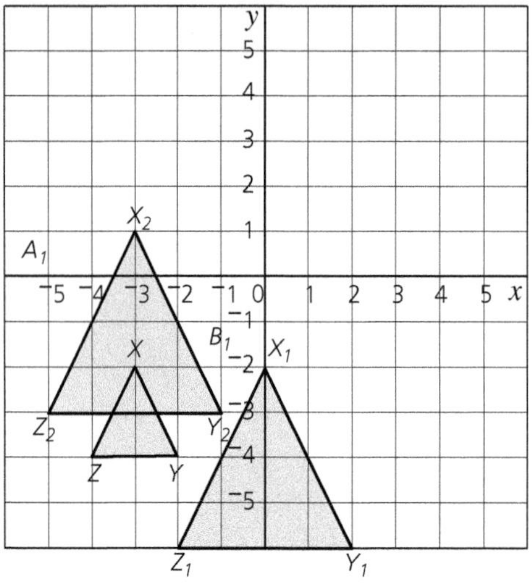

(d) A translation by 3 units left and 3 up

7 (a)–(c)

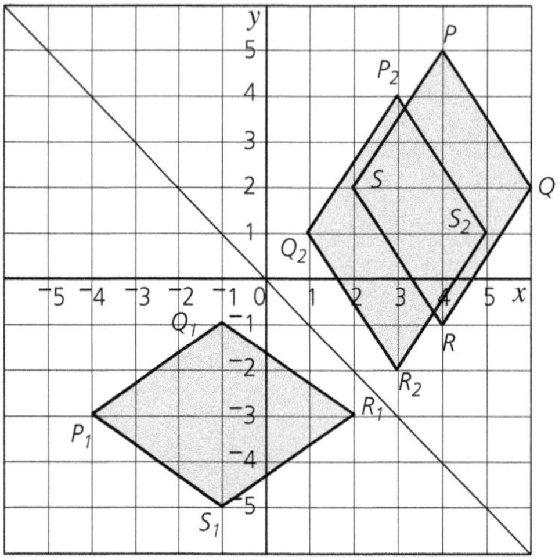

(d) A translation by 1 unit left and 1 down

8 (a)–(c)

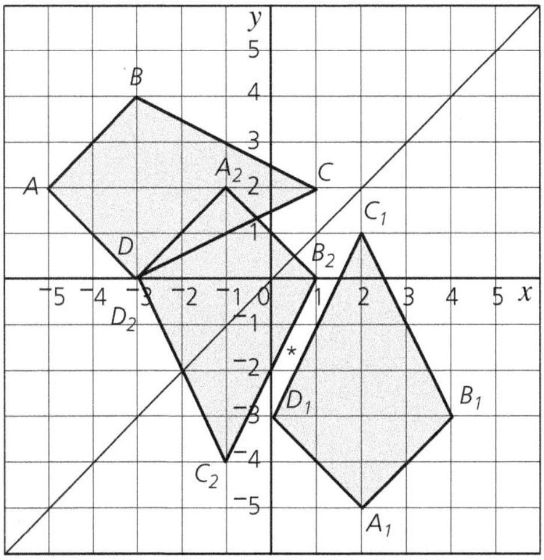

(d) A rotation of 180° about $(\frac{1}{2}, {}^-1\frac{1}{2})$

9 (a)–(c)

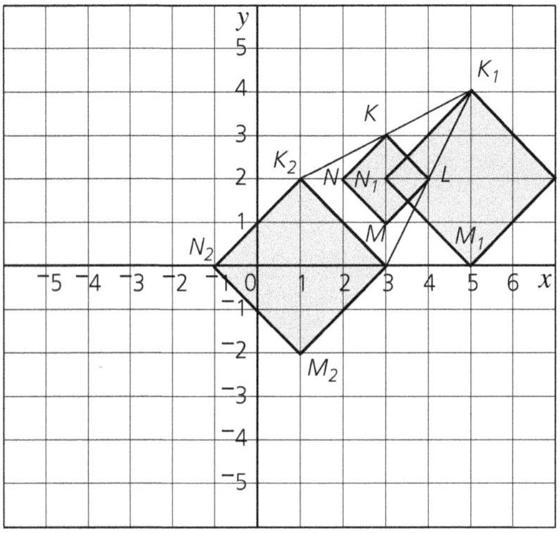

(d) An enlargement by scale factor $\frac{1}{2}$ and centre (5, 4)

10 (a)–(c)

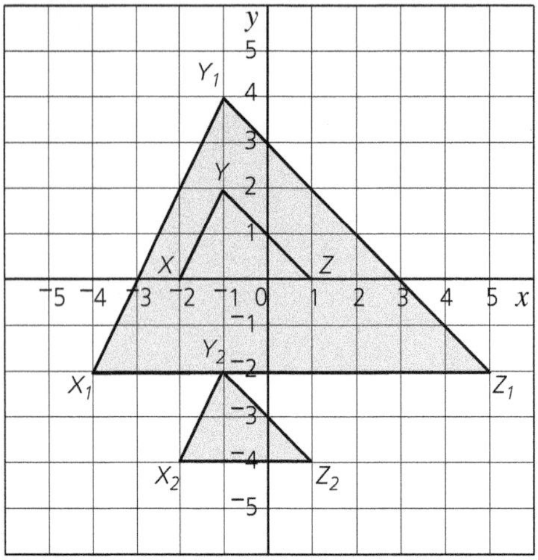

(d) An enlargement by scale factor 3 and centre (⁻1, ⁻5)

Extension Exercise 17.7

1 A reflection in the x-axis

A	A_1	B	B_1
(4, 5)	(4, ⁻5)	(⁻5, 4)	(⁻5, ⁻4)
(5, 1)	(5, ⁻1)	(⁻5, 1)	(⁻5, ⁻1)
(1, 2)	(1, ⁻2)	(⁻2, 2)	(⁻2, ⁻2)
(a, b)	$(a, {}^-b)$	(a, b)	$(a, {}^-b)$

2 A reflection in the y-axis

A	A_2	B	B_2
(4, 5)	(⁻4, 5)	(⁻5, 4)	(5, 4)
(5, 1)	(⁻5, 1)	(⁻5, 1)	(5, 1)
(1, 2)	(⁻1, 2)	(⁻2, 2)	(2, 2)
(a, b)	$({}^-a, b)$	(a, b)	$({}^-a, b)$

3 A reflection in the line $y = x$

A	A_3	B	B_3
(4, 5)	(5, 4)	(⁻5, 4)	(4, ⁻5)
(5, 1)	(1, 5)	(⁻5, 1)	(1, ⁻5)
(1, 2)	(2, 1)	(⁻2, 2)	(2, ⁻2)
(a, b)	(b, a)	(a, b)	(b, a)

4 A reflection in the line $y = {}^-x$

A	A_4	B	B_4
(4, 5)	(⁻5, ⁻4)	(⁻5, 4)	(⁻4, 5)
(5, 1)	(⁻1, ⁻5)	(⁻5, 1)	(⁻1, 5)
(1, 2)	(⁻2, ⁻1)	(⁻2, 2)	(⁻2, 2)
(a, b)	$({}^-b, {}^-a)$	(a, b)	$({}^-b, {}^-a)$

5 A rotation of 90° clockwise about the origin

A	A_1	B	B_1
(4, 5)	(5, ⁻4)	(⁻5, 4)	(4, 5)
(5, 1)	(1, ⁻5)	(⁻5, 1)	(1, 5)
(1, 2)	(2, ⁻1)	(⁻2, 2)	(2, 2)
(a, b)	$(b, {}^-a)$	(a, b)	$(b, {}^-a)$

6 A rotation of 180° about the origin

A	A_2	B	B_2
(4, 5)	(⁻4, ⁻5)	(⁻5, 4)	(5, ⁻4)
(5, 1)	(⁻5, ⁻1)	(⁻5, 1)	(5, ⁻1)
(1, 2)	(⁻1, ⁻2)	(⁻2, 2)	(2, ⁻2)
(a, b)	$({}^-a, {}^-b)$	(a, b)	$({}^-a, {}^-b)$

7 A rotation of 270° clockwise about the origin

A	A_3	B	B_3
(4, 5)	$(^{-}5, 4)$	$(^{-}5, 4)$	$(^{-}4, ^{-}5)$
(5, 1)	$(^{-}1, 5)$	$(^{-}5, 1)$	$(^{-}1, ^{-}5)$
(1, 2)	$(^{-}2, 1)$	$(^{-}2, 2)$	$(^{-}2, ^{-}2)$
(a, b)	$(^{-}b, a)$	(a, b)	$(^{-}b, a)$

8 A rotation of 90° anticlockwise about the origin

A	A_4	B	B_4
(4, 5)	$(^{-}5, 4)$	$(^{-}5, 4)$	$(^{-}4, ^{-}5)$
(5, 1)	$(^{-}1, 5)$	$(^{-}5, 1)$	$(^{-}1, ^{-}5)$
(1, 2)	$(^{-}2, 1)$	$(^{-}2, 2)$	$(^{-}2, ^{-}2)$
(a, b)	$(^{-}b, a)$	(a, b)	$(^{-}b, a)$

9 An enlargement of scale factor 2 and centre of enlargement (0, 0)

A	A_5	B	B_5
(4, 5)	(8, 10)	$(^{-}5, 4)$	$(^{-}10, 8)$
(5, 1)	(10, 2)	$(^{-}5, 1)$	$(^{-}10, 2)$
(1, 2)	(2, 4)	$(^{-}2, 2)$	$(^{-}4, 4)$
(a, b)	$(2a, 2b)$	(a, b)	$(2a, 2b)$

10 Check pupils' own investigations.

Summary Exercise 17.8

1

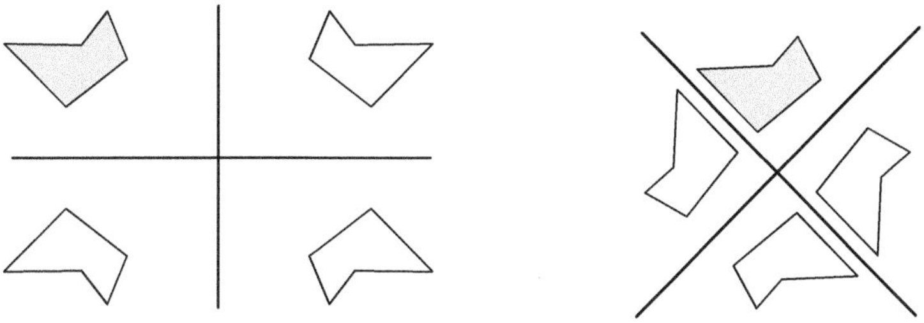

2

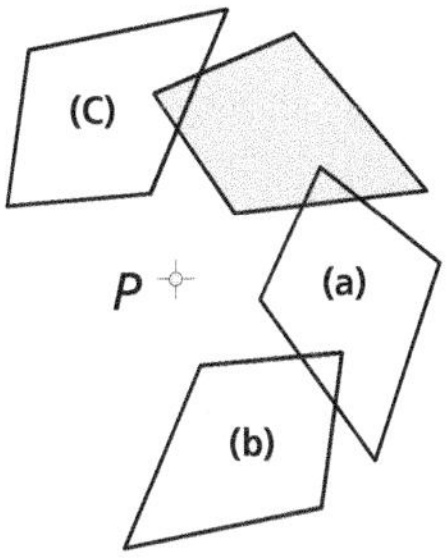

3 (a) (i) 2

(ii) 2

(iii) 4

(iv) none (1)

(v) none (1)

(b) (i) 2

(ii) 2

(iii) 4

(iv) 1

(v) 1

(c)

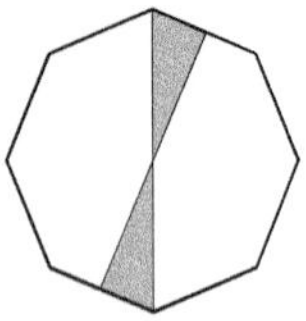

4 (a) A translation by 5 units right and 5 units down

(b) A rotation of 180° about the origin

(c) A reflection in the line $y = x$

(d) An enlargement of scale factor 3 and centre ($^-1$, 1)

5 (a) and (b)

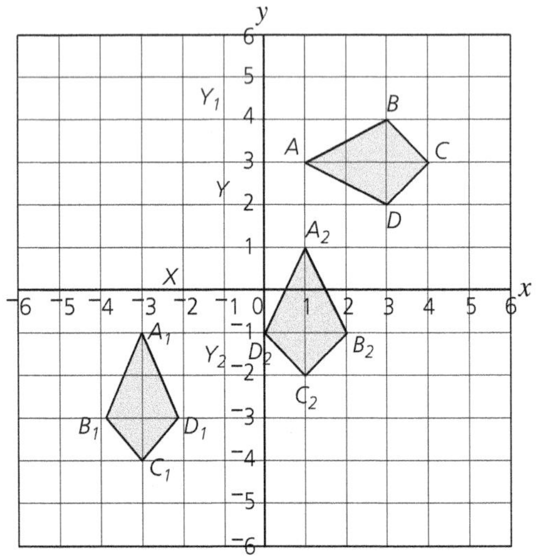

(c) A translation by 4 units right and 2 units up

Activity: Hexaflexagons

Hexaflexagons can be constructed using isometric grid or triangular spotted paper, but it is more fun to get pupils to construct the row of equilateral triangles using their rulers and compasses.

Hexaflexagons are fascinating; your pupils could do some research and see what they can discover about these and other fascinating puzzles.

18 Ratio and proportion

In this chapter we revise all the basics of ratio and proportion before moving on to ratio of areas and volumes after enlargement. Scale drawings by construction are covered followed by scholarship level questions.

Exercise 18.1

1 (a) 35

(b) 24 pink beads, 56 blue beads

(c) 30

2 (a) 270 (b) 288

3 15

4 (a) 4 (b) 36

5 48

6 (a) 2 litres of pineapple juice, 1.5 litres of apple juice, 1 litre of cranberry juice

(b) 4 litres of pineapple juice, 3 litres of apple juice, 2 litres of cranberry juice

7 54°

8 27

9 (a) 5 (b) 6 (c) 10

10 (a) 375 g of flour, 125 g of butter, 250 g of sugar

(b) (i) 1.2 kg (ii) 200 g

Exercise 18.2

1 21

2 $13\frac{1}{3}$

3 22.75 ft

4 63p The exact answer is 62.5p but your pupils should know they need to round up to nearest whole penny.

5 17.5

6 (a) 80 ml (b) 120 ml

7 (a) 196.9 inches

(b) 1.524 m

(c) (i) 20 m (ii) 3 m

8 18 kg

9 (a) 12.5 l (b) 5.5 l

10 (a) 156 g (b) 2 oz

11 (a) 36 000 (b) 50 seconds

12 (a) 16.2 hectares (b) £2914.98

Exercise 18.3

1 (a) 6 cm (b) 36 cm^2 (c) 1 : 4

2 (a) 12 cm (b) 144 cm^2 (c) 1 : 9

3 (a) 12 cm (b) 144 cm^2 (c) 1 : 16

4 (a) 1 cm (b) 1 cm^2 (c) 4 : 1

5 (a) 6 cm and 8 cm (b) 48 cm^2 (c) 1 : 4

6 (a) 15 cm and 18 cm (b) 270 cm^2 (c) 1 : 9

7 (a) 24 cm and 15 cm (b) 180 cm^2 (c) 1 : 9

8 (a) 40 cm (b) 384 cm^2 (c) 1 : 16

9 672 cm^2

10 756 cm^2

11 6 cm

12 6 cm

Exercise 18.4

1 (a) 8 cm^3 (b) 1 : 8

2 (a) 16 cm^3 (b) 1 : 8

3 (a) 8 cm^3 (b) 216 cm^3 (c) 1 : 27

4 (a) 135 cm^3 (b) 1 : 27

5 3 cm^3

6 24 cm^3

Exercise 18.5

1 (a) Check pupils drawing is 14 cm by 22 cm.

(b) (i) 4 cm by 3 cm

(ii) 8.8 cm by 3.4 cm

(iii) 6 cm by 8 cm

2 (a) Smallest jug contains 0.25 litres.

Second contains $0.25 \times 1.25^3 = 0.49$ litres.

Third contains $0.25 \times 1.5^3 = 0.84$ litres.

Fourth contains $0.25 \times 1.75^3 = 1.34$ litres.

Largest contains $0.25 \times 2^3 = 2$ litres.

(b) 15.9 cm (to 1 d.p) volume of 1.0049 litres.

3 (a) 5 m

(b) 250 cm^3

(c) 4 m

4 (a) 2.55 m

(b) 2.55 cm

(c) 200 cm^3

(d) 80 m^2

(e) 80 cm^2

5 (a) 450 cm^2

(b) 120 cm

(c) 1.5 litres

Exercise 18.6

You should briefly revise bearings and constructions before this exercise. Also do carefully show pupils how to draw parallel north lines. They can do this by sliding a set square along a ruler, or more accurately, by constructing the alternate angle.

The scale drawings provided here may not be full size, depending on the scaling of the page.

1 Check pupils' constructions.

Scale is 1 cm to 50 m

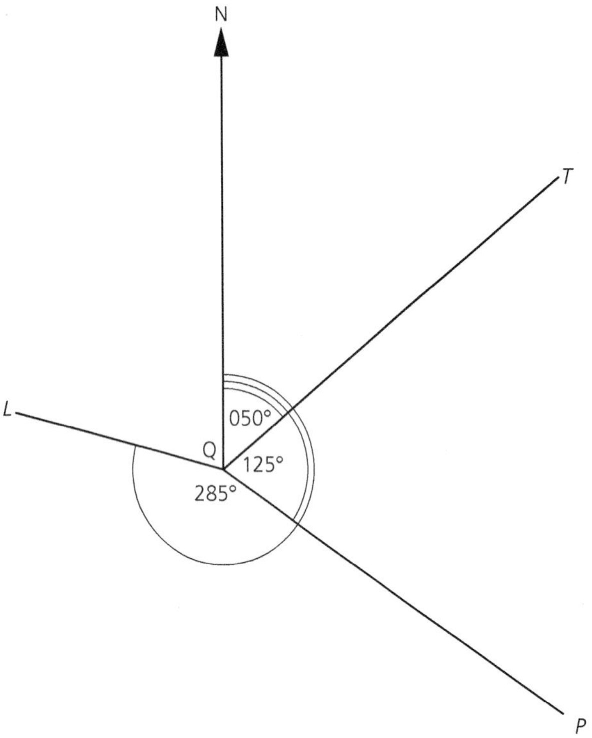

2 Artwork not full size (AB = 6 cm, BC = 5 cm, AC = 5.9 cm

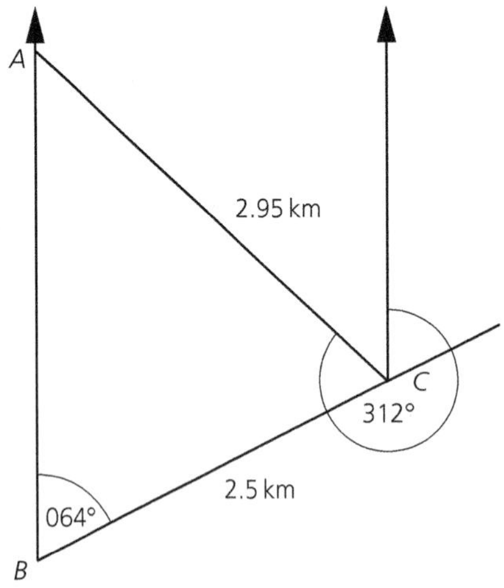

The bearing of *A* from *C* is 312°

The distance is 2.95 km.

3 (a)–(b)

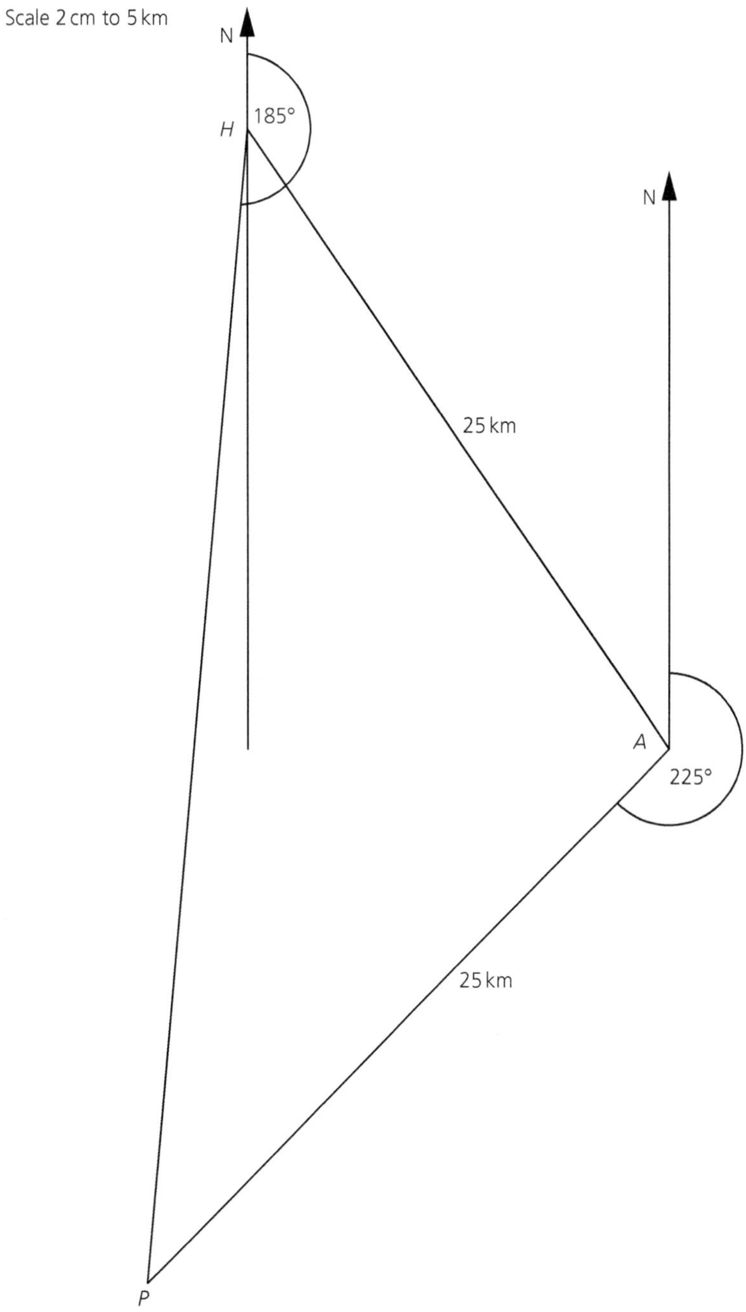

(c) 38.25 km on a bearing of 185°

4 (a)–(b)

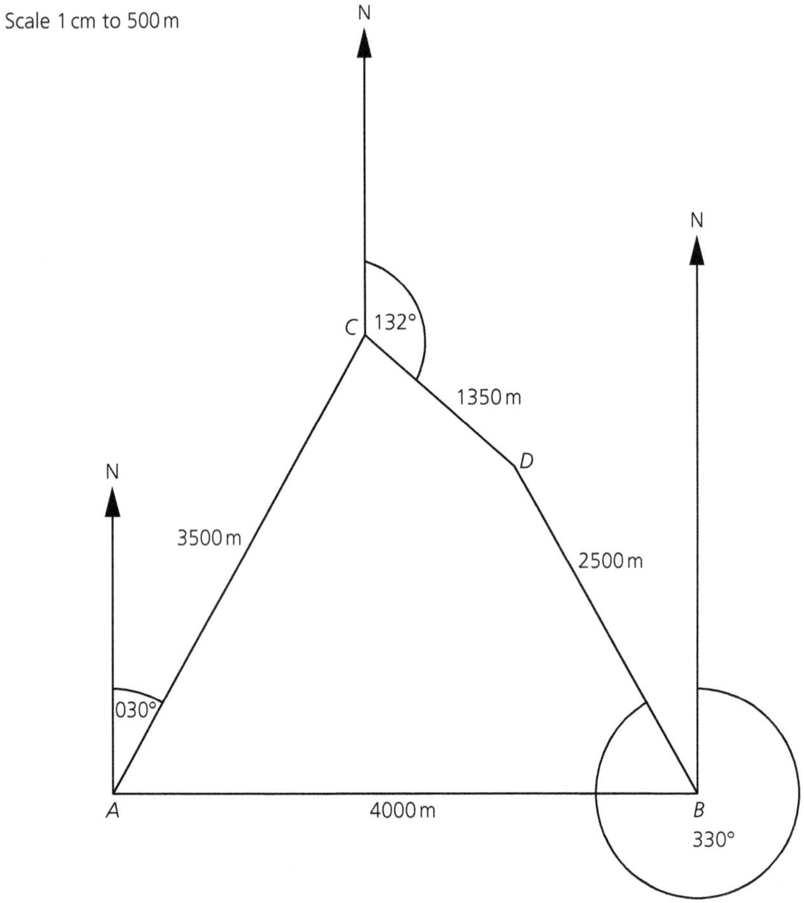

(c) The bearing of D from C is 132°. The distance is 1350 m.

5 (a)

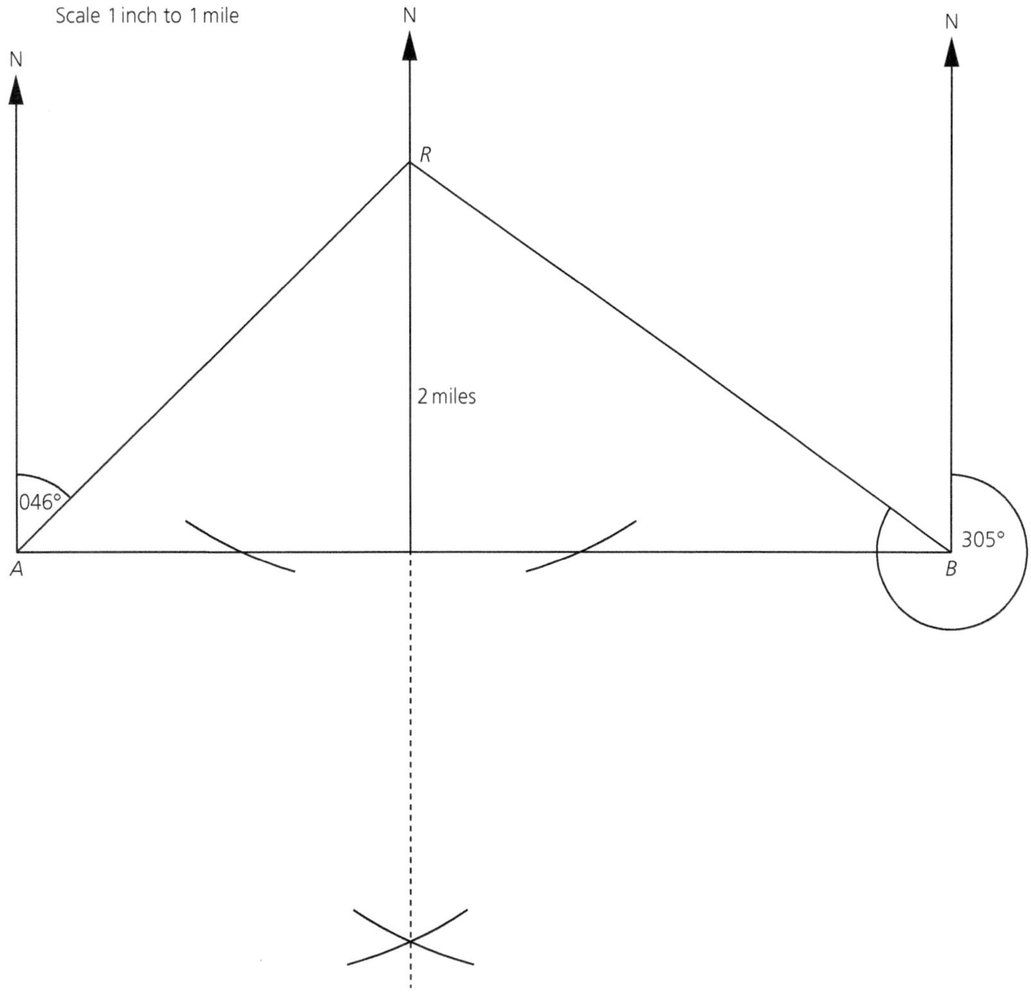

(b) 2 miles

6 Bearing 007°, distance 1900 m

He should have added 180° to 125° to get the correct bearing.

Scale 1 cm to 200 m

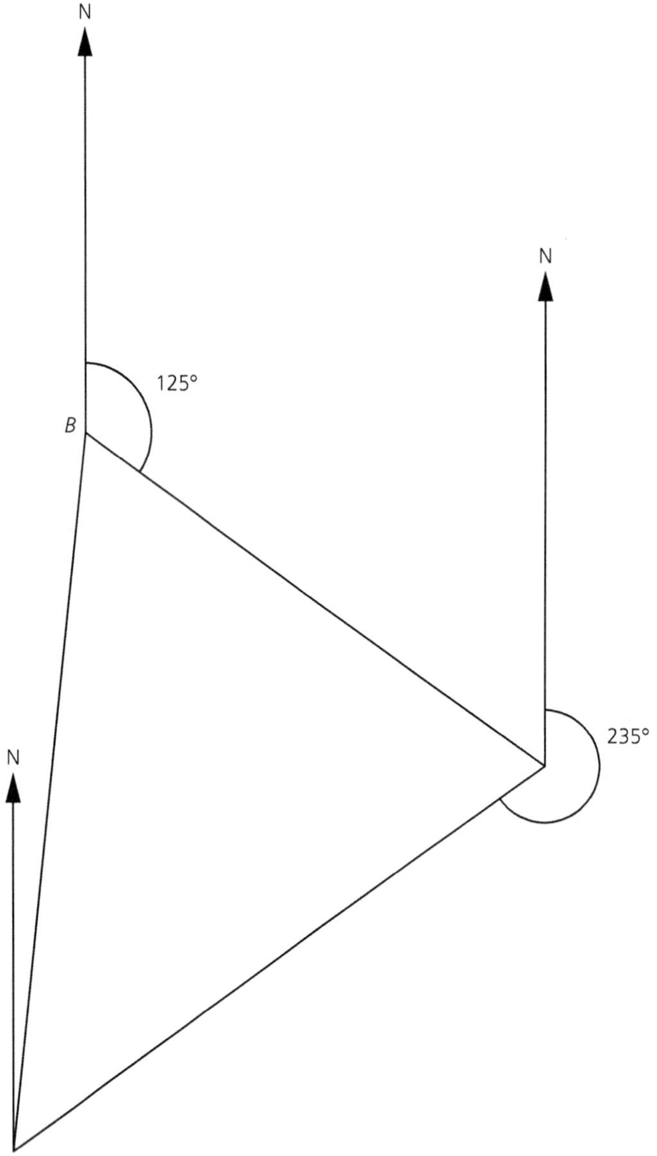

7 (a) (b)

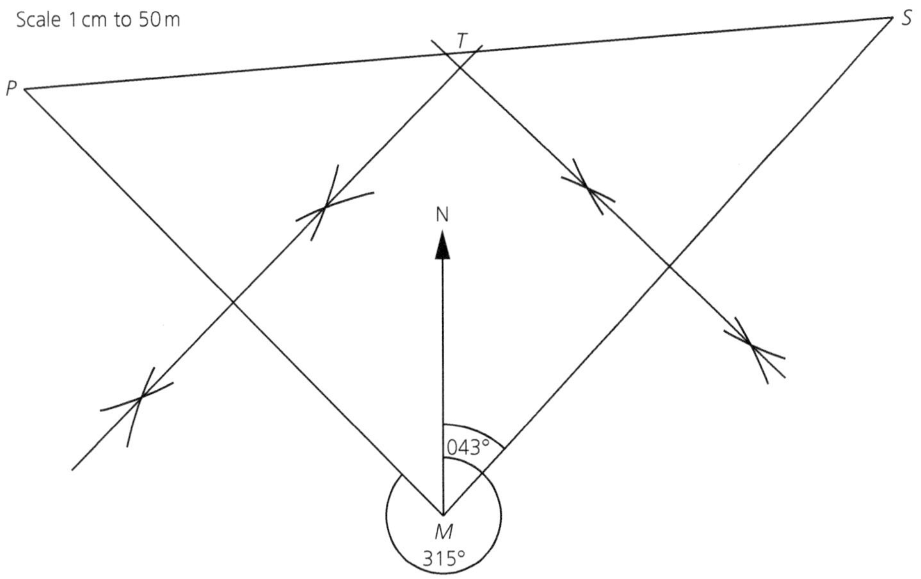

8 Scale 1 cm to $\frac{1}{2}$ Leagues

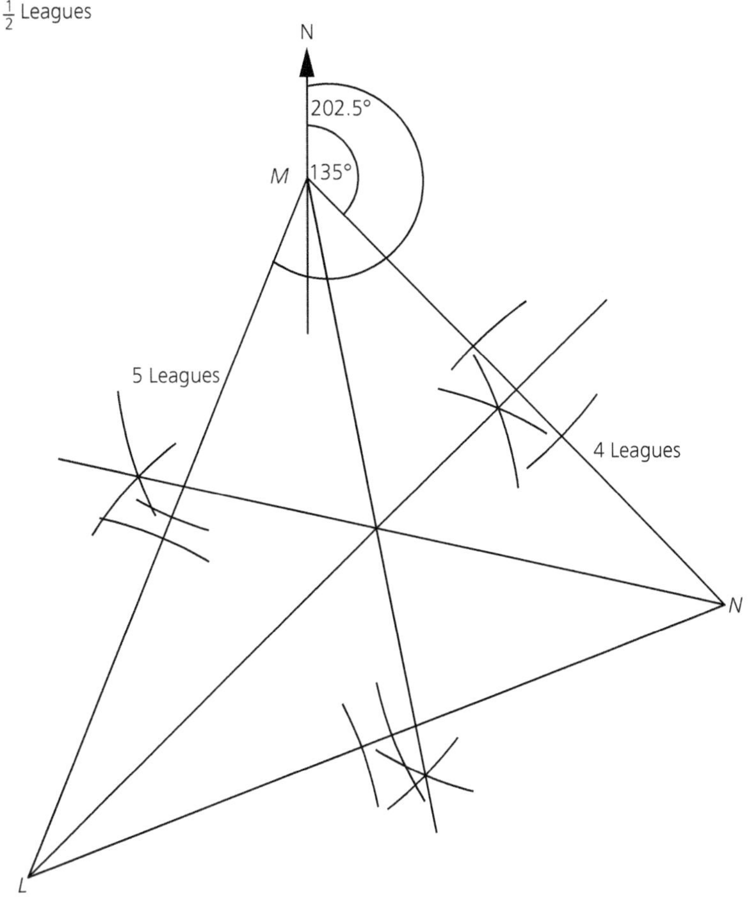

Extension Exercise 18.7

1 **(c)** A pair of spheres and **(e)** a pair of regular tetrahedra

2 125

3 (a) Surface area is $4A$ or $16\pi r^2$ and volume is $8V$ or $\frac{32}{3}\pi r^3$

(b) Surface area is $\frac{4}{9}A$ or $\frac{16}{9}\pi r^2$ and volume is $\frac{8}{27}V$ or $\frac{31}{81}\pi r^3$

(c) (i) Surface area of S : surface area of U is 1 : 9

(ii) Volume S : volume U is 1 : 27

4 (a) $9A$

(b) 1 : 9

(c) $4A$, 1 : 4 : 9

(d) $8V$, $27V$

(e) 1 : 8 : 27

(f) 1 : 7 : 19

5 (a) $32\,\text{cm}^3$

(b) (i) $256\,\text{cm}^3$

(ii) $6912\,\text{cm}^3$

Summary Exercise 18.8

1 (a) 10 cm

(b) $100\,\text{cm}^2$

(c) 1 : 25

2 (a) $27\,\text{cm}^3$

(b) $216\,\text{cm}^3$

(c) 1 : 8

3 $6\,\text{cm}^3$

4 $k = 3, x = 2\frac{2}{3}$ cm, $y = 9$ cm, $z = 27$ cm

5 (a) €35

(b) £28.57

6 (a) Check pupils' drawings.

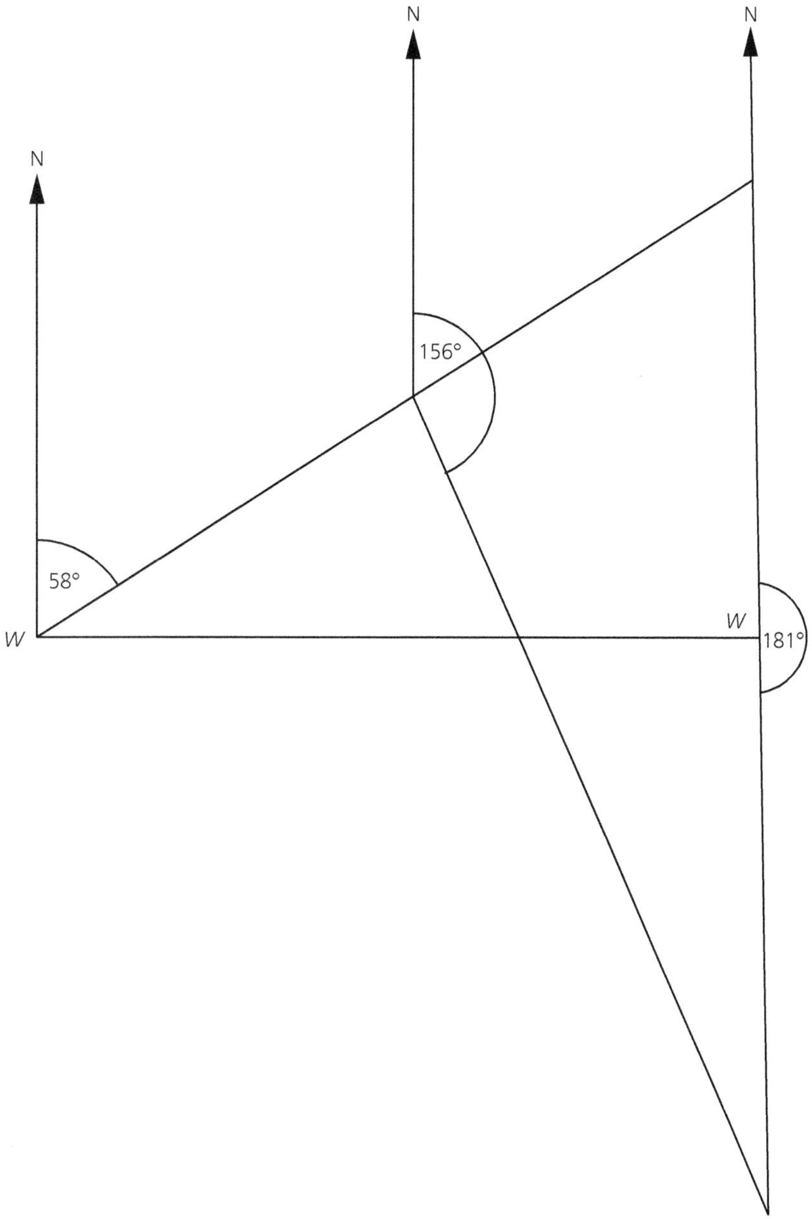

(b) 181° 3.95 km

7 (a) $4h$ cm

(b) $16A$ cm^2

(c) 1 : 64, 1 : 63

Activity: Fibonacci and the golden ratio

Practical

19 Looking at data

In this chapter, pupils revise the methods of looking at data in Mathematics for Common Entrance Book Two. The level of questions is extended to include 'real-life' data, which often does not involve convenient numbers. Pupils should round answers appropriately. It is expected that this chapter will be supported by practical data collection by the pupils.

This chapter may be usefully covered before geography fieldwork. Several of the examples are deliberately based on geography projects.

Exercise 19.1

1 (a) Range = 7 – 1 = 6, mean = $3\frac{1}{3}$, mode = 2, median = 2.5

(b) Range = 2.6 – 1.2 = 1.4, mean = 1.68, mode = 1.2 and 1.5, median = 1.5

(c) Range = 95 – 25 = 70, mean = 64.5, mode none, median = 67

(d) Range = 42 – 34 = 8, mean = 38.6, mode = 37.5, median = 39

2 Check the pupils' own suggestions. Here are some examples:

(a) number of seeds in a grape; scores on an octagonal spinner

(b) increase in height (in cm) grown by bean plants in a week; lengths of beetles (in cm)

(c) ages (in years) of people on a bus; ages (in years) of people in a hospital ward

(d) height (in cm) of newborn baby; time (to the nearest $\frac{1}{2}$ second) of runners in a 200 m race.

3 £147

4 I am 14

5 1.5 m

6 (a) 8 – 3 = 5

(b)

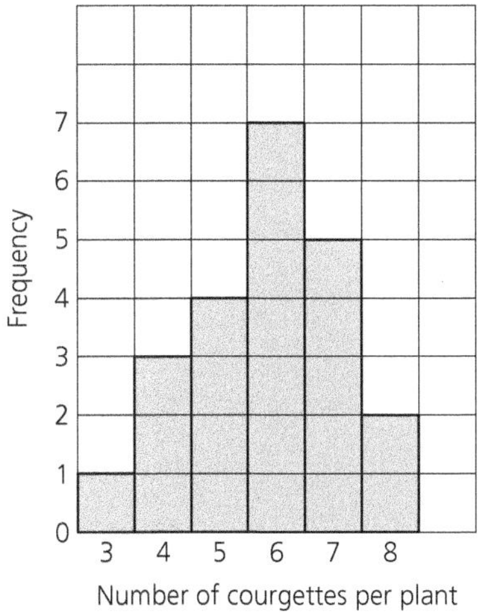

(c) 6 (d) 6 (e) 5.8

7 (a) 16 (b) 2 (c) 2 (d) 2.1

8 (a)

Marks	Tally	Number	Total
9	I	1	9
10			0
11	II	2	22
12	III	3	36
13	I	1	13
14	II	2	28
15	~~IIII~~ II	7	105
16	III	3	48
17	~~IIII~~	5	85
18	II	2	36
19	III	3	57
20	I	1	20
Total		30	459

(b) Range = 20 – 9 = 11, mean = 15.3, mode = 15, median = 15

(c) 13

(d) You cannot, you do not have enough information.

Exercise 19.2

1 (a) Range = 32 – 10 = 22

(b)

Hours	Tally	Frequency
6–10	I	1
11–15	III	3
16–20	~~IIII~~	5
21–25	~~IIII~~ ~~IIII~~	10
26–30	~~IIII~~ III	8
31–35	III	3
Total		30

(c)

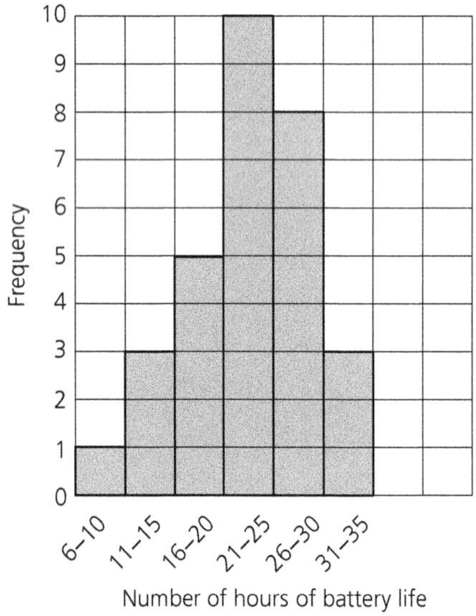

(d) Modal group = 21–25, median = 21– 25, mean = 22.8

2 (a) Range = 3.1 – 0 = 3.1, mean = 1.5, mode = 1.5, median = 1.5

(b)

Rainfall (cm)	Tally	Frequency
0–0.4	~~IIII~~	5
0.5–0.9	II	2
1.0–1.4	~~IIII~~	5
1.5–1.9	~~IIII~~ IIII	9
2.0–2.4	IIII	4
2.5–2.9	IIII	4
3.0–3.4	I	1
		30

A frequency diagram to show the daily rainfall in September

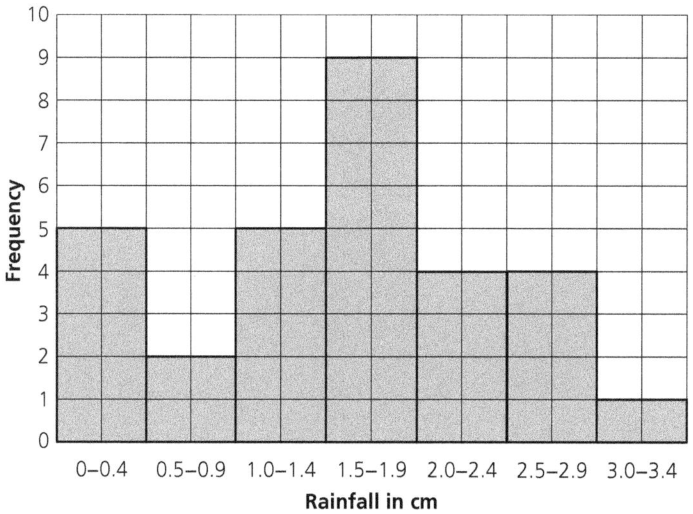

(c) The modal group is 1.5–1.9. The mean, mode and median were all 1.5 cm. It rained on most days.

(d) There was more rainfall than in April, it rained on more days and rained more – the mean rainfall is significantly higher.

3 A frequency table to show the length of time people spent in the park between 7 and 8 in the morning

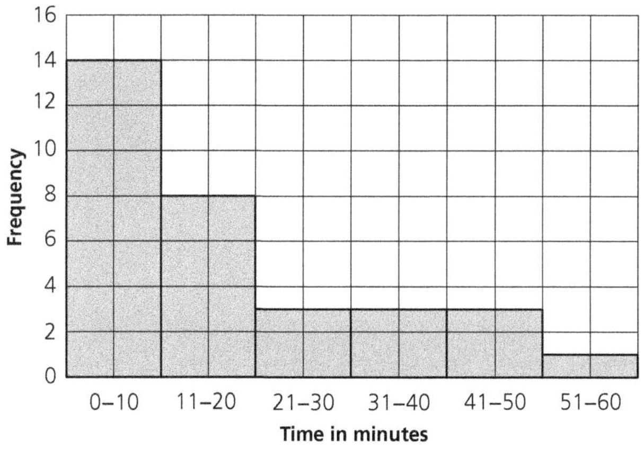

4 A frequency table to show the length of time people spent in the park between 7 and 8 in the early evening

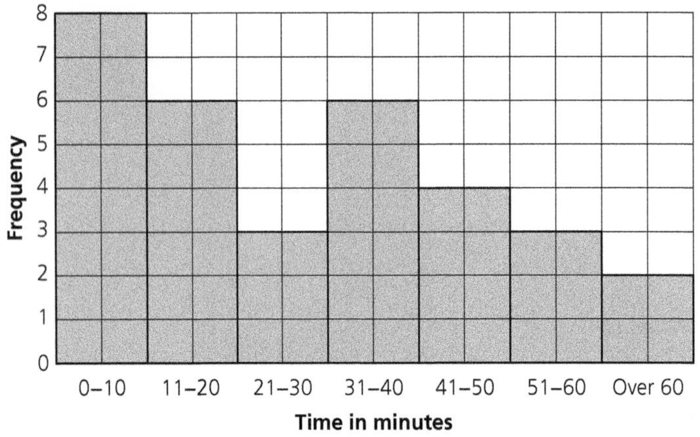

5 In the morning, more people spent shorter periods of time in the park. This may be because they were passing through it on the way to somewhere else (work, shopping, etc.) or it may be small children spending a short time playing in the park.

In the early evening it is more likely that adults would be going to the park, to jog or run, or relax after a day's work. Older children might go to play football. Probably fewer people would come and just sit because it might be cooler.

6 (a) A frequency diagram to show the results of a survey that looked at the ages of passengers taking the Eurostar train to Paris on a weekday

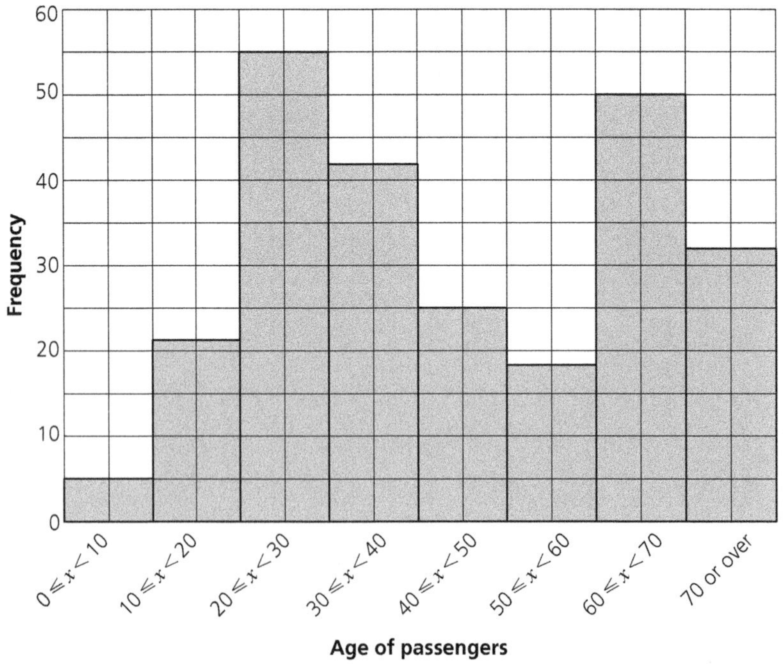

(b) They would be at school or college.

(c) Perhaps there are special discount for over 60s. They also have more free time.

7 (a) The results of a survey that looked at the ages of passengers taking the Eurostar train to Paris at the weekend

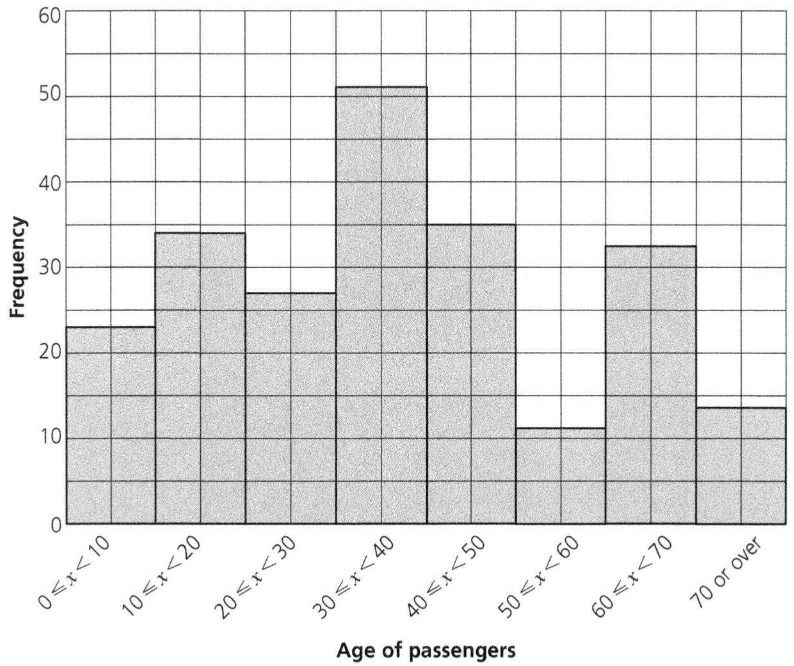

(b) There are more young passengers and fewer old ones.

Exercise 19.3

1

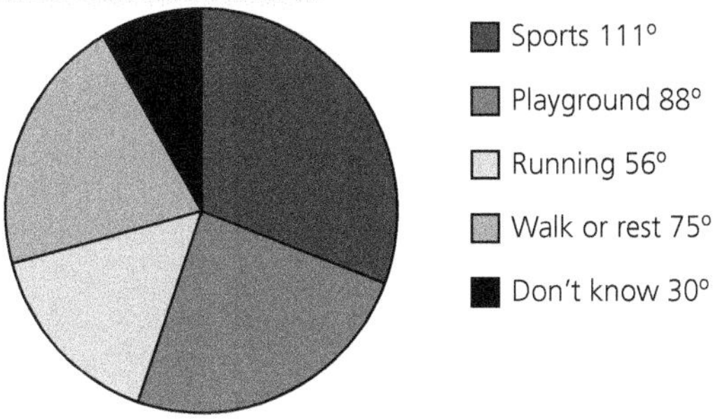

Reason for going to the park

2

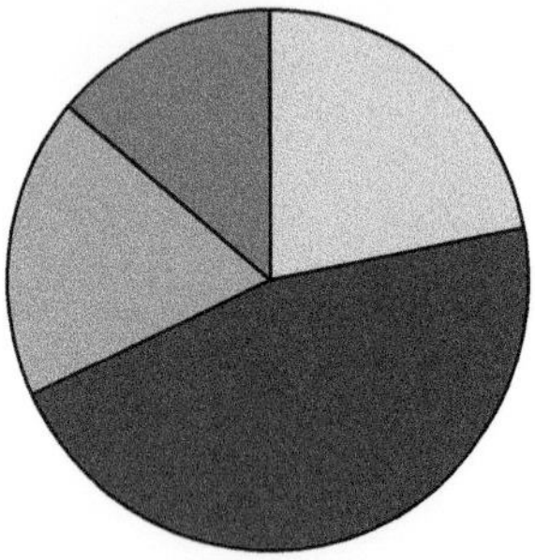

Sales at the park pavilion

3 (a)–(b)

Number of seeds	Frequency	Angle
2	2	14°
3	10	72°
4	13	94°
5	16	115°
6	6	43°
7	3	22°
Total	50	360°

(c)

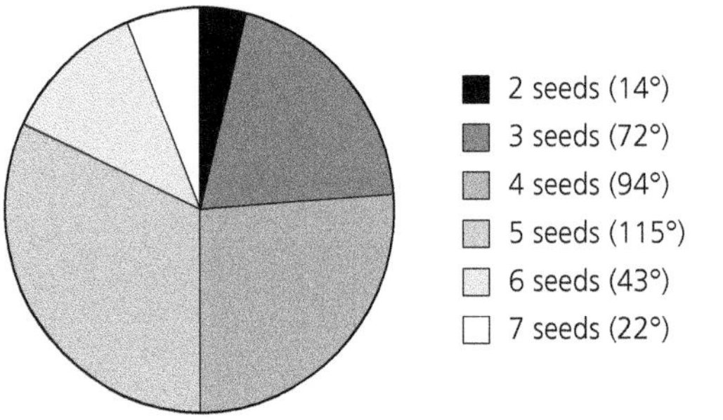

A pie chart to show the numbers of seeds found in seed pods

(d) The mode was 5 seeds, most had 4, 5 or 6 seeds, a few had 2 or 3, and a few had 7

4 The range of the number of seeds was less (5) in the wetter environment.

The mode and the median in the wetter environment was 2, in the drier environment the mode was 5 and the median 4.5 and the mean was 4.46. (They cannot calculate the mean in the wetter environment.)

5 (a) 40
(b) 12
(c) 2
(d) 4
(e) 4
(f) 3.65
(g) 194 books

Exercise 19.4

1 (a) 41
(b) 146 cm

2 (a)

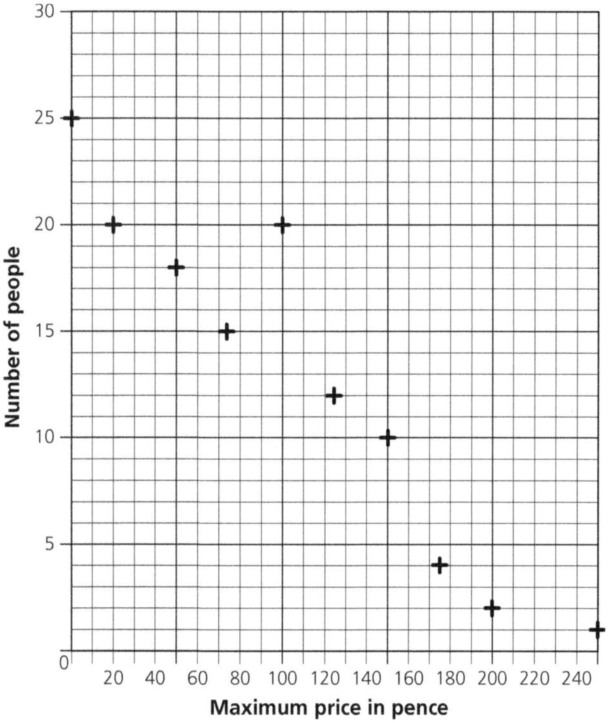

A scatter graph to show the results of our survey to find out the maximum price people would consider paying in order to go into the park

(b) The graph shows negative correlation.

3 **(a)** A scatter graph to show the results of a survey looking at the recorded midday temperatures and the number of people who used the park in the early evening

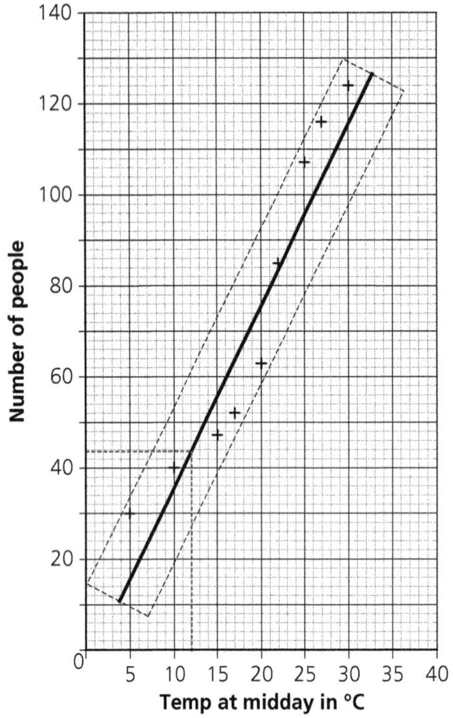

(b) Check the line of best fit.

(c) Positive correlation.

(d) 44 people

4 (a) A scatter graph to compare the number of hours spent revising to the positions achieved in the examinations

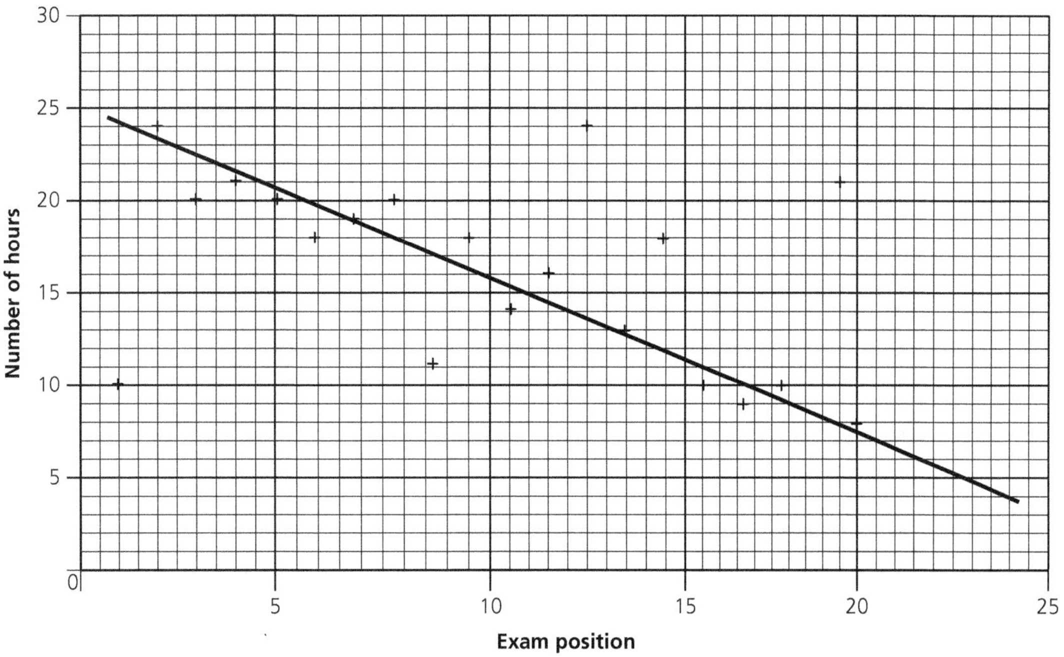

(b) The graph shows a negative correlation. The smaller the amount of revision done, the lower the exam position achieved. Note that pupils may draw the graph with the examination position on the vertical axis and number of hours on the horizontal axis.

(c) About 9th

(d) The person who came top with ten hours revision could have just been an exceptional pupil. Some people might revise for a long time but still not be able to remember what they know in examinations. Some people might not tell the truth (it is uncool to be seen to be working hard). Other reasons could be illness during the examination, revision of the wrong material or poor revision technique.

Extension Exercise 19.5

1 (a) 6, 6, 8, 10; only one possible answer

(b) 6, 8, 14, 16, 16; only one possible answer

2

Number in house	Tally	Frequency	Total people
2	II	2	$2 \times 2 = 4$
3	IIII	4	$3 \times 4 = 12$
4	~~IIII~~ III	8	$4 \times 8 = 32$
5	~~IIII~~ II	7	$5 \times 7 = 35$
6	III	3	$6 \times 3 = 18$
7	1	1	$7 \times 1 = 7$
	Total	25	108

Mean $= \frac{108}{25} = 4.32$, mode = 4, median = 4

3 (a) (i) If $x = 8$, mode = 4, median = 4

(ii) If $x = 9$, mode = 3 and 4, median = 3.5

(iii) If $x = 10$, mode = 3, median = 3

(b) $x = 5$, mode = 4, median = 4

4 (a) 20 and 25

(b) 25 minutes

(c) 23 minutes

(d)

Time (minutes)	Frequency
0–5	7
6–10	17
11–15	17
16–20	20
21–25	17
26–30	14
31–35	12
36–40	11
41–45	9
46–50	7
51–55	5
56–60	2
Total	138

(e) A frequency diagram to show the journey times to school

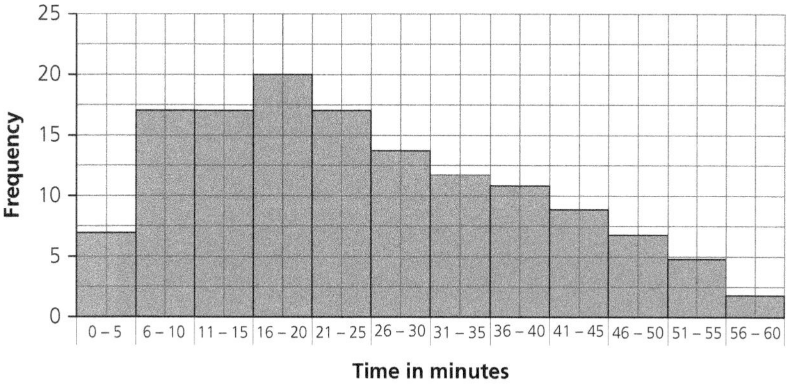

(f) 138

(g) 16–20 minutes

5 (a) Holidays usually go in weeks and a week is 7 days.

(b) One who comes from abroad, like an Australian or a young teacher who likes travelling.

(c) 12.96 days

(d) 13.92 days

6 (a) A frequency chart to show the amount of money raised in a Readathon

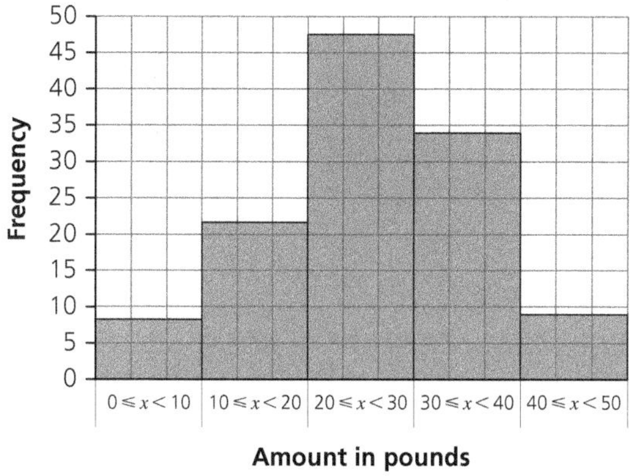

(b) $5 \times 8 + 15 \times 22 + 25 \times 47 + 35 \times 34 + 45 \times 9 = £3140$

Summary Exercise 19.6

1 (a) Range = 5 − 1 = 4, mean = 2.6, median = 2.5, mode = 1

(b) Range = 5.8 − 1.2 = 4.6, mean = 3.8, median = 4.2, mode = 4.2

(c) Range = $3\frac{1}{2} - 1\frac{3}{4} = 1\frac{3}{4}$, mean = 2.65, median = $2\frac{1}{2}$, mode none

2 (a) 12 minutes 12 seconds

(b) 11 minutes 58 seconds

3 (a)

Height (cm)	Frequency
0–9	5
10–19	3
20–29	9
30–39	9
40–49	4
Total	30

A frequency chart to show the heights of bean plants

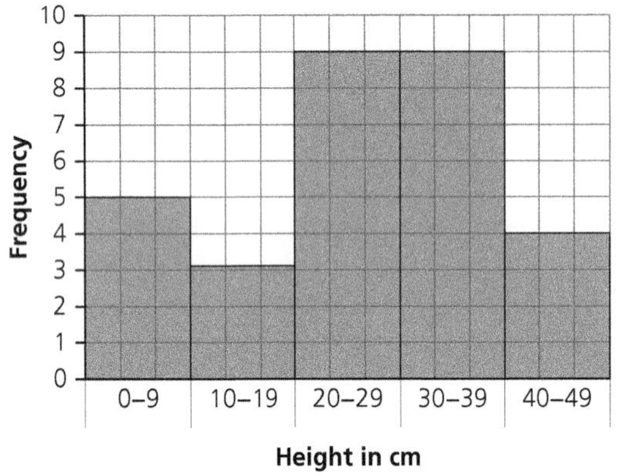

Range = 48 – 0 = 48, mean = 25.5, median = 26.5, modal group = 20–29 and 30–39

(b) Most plants grew well, in a small range of 23–48, 5 did not grow at all and 3 grew less than 20 cm.

(c) The modal group does not change, the mean becomes 30.6 and the median is 31

(d) Yes, the plants should be included in the results. It is important to know that some plants may not grow.

4 (a)

Opinion	Frequency	Angle (°)
Very satisfied	30	63
Satisfied	42	89
Neither satisfied or dissatisfied	58	123
Dissatisfied	24	51
Very dissatisfied	16	34
Total	170	360

(b)

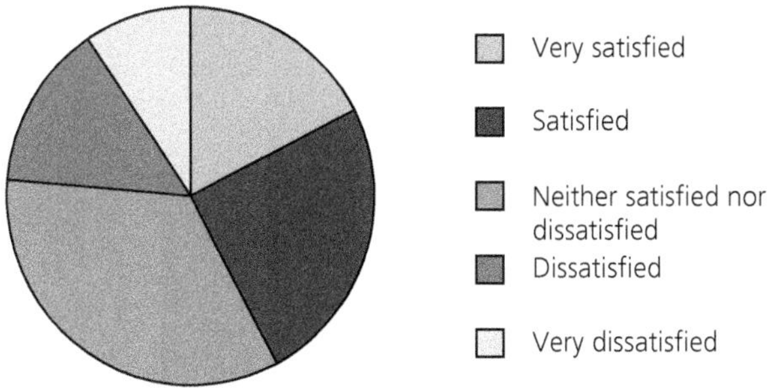

Pupil Satisfaction with school lunches

(c) 23.5%

5 (a)–(b) Predicted vs highest actual temperatures

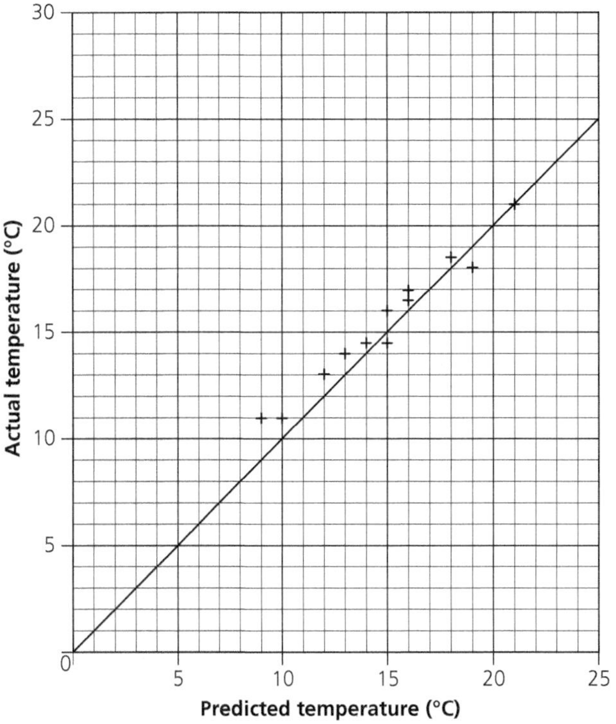

(c) 10.5

6 Mean = 20 351, mode = 14 000, median = 18 000

(a) Mean – but it depends on your salary

(b) Median

(c) Mean

Activity: Marketing the school

Hopefully a useful exercise for the school and a productive project for the pupils. Wish them well from all of us at Galore Park!